RICHARD LA RUINA was born in London in 1980. Always shy and reserved, he moved to Cambridge with his mother aged twelve. Although his own teachers considered him an underachiever, Richard's initial ambition was to be a primary school teacher. However, he soon discovered the stock market, buying his first shares after his eighteenth birthday. This led to five years of trading from home. It was both a gift and a curse, making him enough money to travel the world while he completely neglected his social life. At twenty-one Richard had never kissed a girl, or even been on a date. His first relationship lasted two-and-a-half years, which granted him some much-needed confidence with women. From this point, he resolved to boost his self-esteem by improving his fashion sense and body language, while engaging in activities like public speaking and salsa dancing to develop confidence. After moving back to London, Richard joined the international 'pick-up artist' community, meeting literally hundreds of women each month to enhance his seduction skills and make up for lost time. He soon realised he was perfectly placed to teach these skills, setting up a website to offer one-to-one training. In 2007 he set up PUATraining.com, the only British company of its type, whose staff have already trained hundreds of students.

THE
NATURAL
ART OF
SEDUCTION
Secrets of Success with Women

RICHARD LA RUINA

First published in paperback 2007
Revised edition first published in paperback 2009
By Pennant Books

British Library Cataloguing-in-Publication Data:
A catalogue record for this book is available from
The British Library

ISBN 978-1-906015-13-8

Design & Typeset by Envy Design Ltd

Printed by Thomson Litho, East Kilbride, Scotland

5 7 9 10 8 6

Pictures reproduced with kind permission of the author.

*Every reasonable effort has been made to acknowledge the ownership of copyright
material included in this book. Any errors that have inadvertently occurred will be
corrected in subsequent editions provided notification is sent to the publisher.*

Pennant Books
A division of Pennant Publishing Ltd
PO Box 5675
London W1A 3FB
www.pennantbooks.com

Contents

Introduction

MY FULL-TIME JOB IS TEACHING MEN HOW TO BE GOOD WITH WOMEN. I run a company called PUA Training.com, the largest of its kind in Europe. 'PUA' stands for 'Pick-Up Artist', the term for someone skilled in meeting, attracting and seducing women. I'm the best seducer in Europe, and I'm great at taking a guy with no skill with ladies whatsoever and turning him into a cool, confident guy who can get all the girls he wants.

This book outlines every necessary element for maximising your chances of success, and minimising your chances of cringe-worthy moments at every step of an interaction. It was an amazing day for me when I first discovered I could *learn* how to be great with women, that I wasn't destined to always be the guy who could never get the girl. This isn't the kind of thing you can learn in your house – real people are going to observe you as you learn – but this barrier is what will hold back the majority of men and allow *you* to stand out.

I've dedicated the past few years to this area, first by working on myself, and then by helping others to follow the same steps. All the material in this book is tried, tested and proven to work. It has worked for people from all over the world, of all ages and all backgrounds.

The knee-jerk reaction is to imagine that this stuff is for losers and geeks, that real men don't need it. But think about it: how many guys do you know who could get pretty much any woman they wanted? In *any* situation?

It's an area at the core of the male ego, and it takes strength to admit that this is somewhere that you could improve. The great thing is that, if you are humble enough to admit this and put some time in, you'll soon overtake the cocky guys who like to think they have nothing to learn.

This is a new area of study. For years, people have developed different methods of learning skills. You can take piano lessons or learn to drive a car: the common element is that someone who already knows how to do something teaches you how to do it too. They know how to teach their subject, and they know how someone can learn. Being good with women is no different; it's just taken a lot longer for people to realise that the skills that some possess naturally can be learned by others, and to find a way to clearly communicate them.

It's taken so long because most guys who are naturally good don't know how to communicate it to others. Women, I'm sorry to say, aren't usually the best to ask for advice: "just be funny" or "just be confident" aren't particularly helpful. (I certainly didn't know what to do with that advice.)

I can guarantee that, if you read this book and apply what you learn, you *will* be better with women. This isn't a scientific textbook in the sense of collecting statistics and doing phone surveys. Everything I have written is from my own experience and has been tried and tested in the best lab for human interaction – the real world: the coffee shops, streets, bars and clubs of London. Human interaction is not something that can be studied from the sidelines. You can't teach seduction techniques or theorise about it without talking to real women in real situations. But what is within these pages will work for you. You will be able to look back at your previous interactions with the benefit of this new knowledge, and see how you could have been more successful.

How to Read This Book

YOU WILL BENEFIT MOST FROM THIS BOOK IF YOU READ IT IN ORDER. IT IS LAID OUT IN A LOGICAL SEQUENCE TO TAKE YOU THROUGH THE NECESSARY ELEMENTS OF AN INTERACTION, ALL THE WAY TO THE 'CLOSE'. I have placed 'inner game' (the mental attitudes and beliefs that will make you more attractive) last, because it's something you can work on in conjunction with your interaction skills – I want you to be out there practising as much as possible, not using the excuse of not having got past the inner game chapter to stop you going out!

A certain amount of you will read the book and not actively put the methods to use. You'll still do slightly better, because the information will be in your mind and any interactions you have will go more smoothly than before you had the knowledge.

The guys who achieve the most will be going out and putting my methods to use. They will be determined to try each new thing they learn and will be out many nights a week. They will put the theory into practice, looking at the results and refining their approach for the next time.

Glossary

IN THIS BOOK, I USE A SMALL AMOUNT OF SEDUCTION-SPECIFIC TERMS. There is a 'seduction community', groups of guys who post on message boards on specific websites, who meet in bars and clubs in the major cities of the world with the goal of developing better skills with women. I've never been part of this community, finding message boards a bad way to learn how to interact with people in live situations, but the terms originally used by these guys have filtered more and more into the mainstream. I'll use those that make it easier to explain certain concepts, whilst trying not to sound too geeky!

AMOG: Alpha Male of Group/Alpha Male Other Guy.
Closing: Getting a number or a physical 'close' (the end result of an interaction).
Direct/Indirect: Showing interest straight away/coming in under the radar once the group is disarmed and the target starts to give indicators of interest.
High Value: A high-value girl could be a celebrity, at the extreme end, or just a girl who stands out in her

environment: a barmaid (hit on all the time), a stripper, a model – basically the one that all men want. The high-value male has status – he might be the owner of a club, a millionaire or someone in a similarly desirable position.

IOI: Indicator of Interest (girl showing she likes you).

In-Set: In an interaction with the girl or group that you have opened.

Kino: Touching.

Mixed Set: Group containing men.

Natural: Guy who is naturally very successful with women (the 'other ten per cent').

Opener: The first thing you say.

Routine Stack: A sequence of scripted and memorised material.

Set: Group of girls (e.g. two-set, three-set).

Social Proof: Increasing your attractiveness within a certain location by being seen to know and talk to everyone, or getting attention from other women. Body language and demeanour may also raise your social value.

Target: The girl in the set that you are interested in.

Wingman: Someone who goes out with you to meet women.

Background – Zero to Hero, My Story

I DEVELOPED THE SYSTEM OVER MANY YEARS OF THEORY AND PRACTICE. WHAT I'VE PUT TOGETHER IS A SYSTEM FOR BECOMING A 'NATURAL', A MAN WHO WOMEN FIND NATURALLY ATTRACTIVE WITHOUT HIM USING ANY ROUTINES OR GIMMICKS. Of course, I have a huge collection of routines and tricks, from palm reading to Derren Brown-style mind tricks. These things work and I'll teach some to you. However, what the System allows you to do is to use your own personality and natural attractiveness as a base, thereby reducing the need to rely on pre-programmed material. Chat-up lines, routines and gimmicks give you something to fall back on, something that you can use in the early days when you run out of things to say. It's like using training wheels whilst you develop your natural confidence.

I was an extremely shy and introverted guy. I wasn't a

geek, but I *was* a loser in terms of social interaction. Up until the age of twenty-one, I hadn't had any success with women whatsoever – not even a kiss! What held me back were these simple things:

- I was very bad socially; meeting new people scared me, and I avoided it. I was the guy at social events who everyone asked, "What's wrong?" or "Are you okay?"
- I had low self-esteem, a bad self-image and was even clinically depressed at one time.
- I was nervous, shy and socially un-calibrated – I often annoyed people by saying the wrong things.
- I was called 'ugly' all through school and college.
- People made fun of my voice, so I was scared to speak loudly, or in public, and even avoided making phone calls.

As an introvert, I had a few close friends rather than a big social circle. My friends would invite me out to parties and clubs all the time, but I never went. The older I got, the more of a constant worry it became. Any girl I met would be more experienced than me, and it would be embarrassing. I wondered if I'd ever meet anyone. At the same time, I was moderately successful in terms of my career. This would have been a surprise to my school teachers, who were certain I'd be a failure. I'd proven good at marketing, and even gained a skill in trading on the stock market in my spare time. I wasn't going to be a millionaire, but for the first time I was recognised as intelligent and hard working.

To enable you to fully appreciate my difficulties with women, here are some of my worst moments from the ages of sixteen to twenty-one:

- In college there was a girl who obviously fancied me, and I fancied her. Why she did, I have no idea – she was certainly the only one who did at the time. I spent the whole year trying to pluck up the courage to say something as simple as, "Hello, how are you doing?" but never did. It wouldn't have been too difficult – she was sitting next to me most of the time. One day I left a note on her bike to say that I liked her, and that we should go on a date. Yes, I am very embarrassed to admit it – and, no, it didn't work.

- In university, a hot girl who I lived with in halls was tipsy one night. She came to me and said, "Richard, I'm really horny!" She was beautiful and I'd been hugely attracted to her since the first moment I saw her. We got on as friends, and I guess I was just in the right place at the right time to take things further. I handled it in the most wimpy way possible; I said, "Oh dear," patted her arm and made an excuse to leave. I didn't have much regret about that at the time; I didn't know how to kiss her properly, never mind how to take things to a sexual level. She had a bemused look on her face, and mentioned some time later that she thought I must have been a virgin. For a long time I regretted not taking advantage of those university years, when it *is* a lot easier to hook up with girls.

- One day in the street, two girls came over and one said, "You look like her ex-boyfriend." They were giving me a lot of attention, but I said, "Oh really?" and let the conversation stale out.

- One day on a train, a group of girls started talking to me and asked if I'd ever had a threesome. I didn't have enough courage to ask for their phone number. Instead, I let them leave.

- At a bar one night, a girl came and said, "Would you like to lick my lizard?" She showed me the lizard tattoo on her belly; I did lick it, and she stood there expectantly. I said nothing and she left. I just wasn't thinking of sex at all, it was way too far removed from my current situation. I wanted to hold hands, hug, kiss – basically to have a girlfriend. Overtly sexual girls scared me because I knew I couldn't handle them at all.

I can look back now at all the times I've left women with a bemused look on their faces, thinking, "What was wrong with that guy?"

THE STORY CONTINUES

In September 2001, a friend invited me out to a club and I uncharacteristically agreed to go. The night before, I'd almost sold my soul to the devil, saying I'd give up all my material possessions for a girl. A funny thing happened in the car: he wanted to go to a certain club, but I insisted on another one. This was uncharacteristic too, since I generally deferred to my friends. In the club I'd chosen, my friend was approached by a hot girl. I stood there watching as he chatted with her. After a couple of minutes, her friend returned from the dance-floor. Our friends were quickly getting closer, and were oblivious to us. I can't remember who spoke first, but we got into a boring conversation and I bought her a drink. Because we were forced together, she had to talk with me for an hour or more. I was nervous, and couldn't hold good eye contact, but I guess she liked my nice-guy manner. My friend and the other girl were getting on so well that he was taking her back to his place. He wanted to drop us off home first, so we went to my girl's street, said goodbye and she got out of the car. She walked five metres; I was paralysed. I gripped the car seat, and then had one of those life-changing moments when you force yourself to take action – I told my friend to wait and ran after her. I called her name; she turned and I said, "Can I have your number?" She gave it. This was the first time I'd ever got a girl's number!

The next day, I didn't call my prized number because I was too nervous. I called the day after, but she didn't answer. I was immediately heartbroken; she obviously had better things to do than speak to a loser like me, it can only have been because her friend had deserted her that she talked to me in the first place. Amazingly, though, she called me back a couple of hours later! She had been at work. We arranged to meet for drinks in a couple of days. We had a few dates after that, and they were pretty crazy – she brought her ugly friend along on the first and tried to set us up. On the second, I cooked dinner at my place. Afterwards, she sat next to me on the couch, put her head on my shoulder and I . . . stroked her hair!

On the third date, I find out she has a boyfriend. By now, I'm not working on the stock market during the day any more – my full-time job is trying to get this girl to be my girlfriend. We meet in the day for the first time, and I'm sure she'll find me ugly in the daylight. But she dumps her boyfriend, since it's a long-distance relationship and isn't really working. Next though, she is going to university: a four-hour train ride away, but I book a hotel room for her first week and arrange to visit every weekend.

It took me three dates to kiss her, and after ten dates we still hadn't slept together.

To cut a long story short, I work to overcome all the obstacles and, for some crazy reason, my desperate neediness doesn't scare her off. We spend the next two and a half years together. I'm happy and in love, and give up pretty much all my other interests. After two years we start to have problems; I've changed a lot, she has too, and we start to argue more and more over the next six months. Things deteriorate and we mutually agree to break up.

It's March 2004, and I'm single again. But I think meeting girls is a cinch, because I'm more confident and have a one hundred per cent open-close record in clubs! Over the next couple of years I make some approaches, get some numbers, have a few dates and they *all* stale out without me getting any more kisses.

Over the same time, I was doing a lot of self-improvement. I wrote down all my problems, all the ways in which I wanted to be better, and made a plan for addressing each one. For my shyness, I decided to do a TEFL (Teaching English as a Foreign Language) course in Seville, Spain. This is what a lot of people who love travel choose to do, as it qualifies the person as a teacher of English to foreign students. It forced me to be the centre of attention and stand up in front of a class of people for an hour at a time. In my first class, I was nervous and my voice was shaking. By the last one I was pretty good. Much of getting over shyness, and even fear, in approaching women relies on desensitisation. The course helped me a lot.

I started reading two self-improvement books a week. I studied Neuro-Linguistic Programming (NLP), which is a branch of psychology that uses different techniques such as the artful use of language and visualisation to influence our subconscious minds, and the subconscious minds of others. It can be used to remove limiting beliefs, to cure phobias and to get on better with other people. Some people make outlandish claims for NLP, such as its being able to speed up your metabolism to lose weight, or even to create time distortion in martial arts, so that you can see the other person in slow motion and kick their ass, *Matrix* style! They take things too far: as pretty much anyone can set themselves up as an NLP guru, you need to take the more farfetched claims

salt. Still, it has some very powerful and easy-
ques that were a big help to me.

studied mainstream psychology, hypnosis,
Buddhism and other self-development texts. I didn't
anticipate the effect this would have, but it made me calmer
and more composed, generally happier and more
contented. Buddhism and hypnosis made my focus of
attention internal. These books were the perfect antidote to
watching videos on MTV with hot women, the ones that
make us even more unsatisfied with our lives. I also took
various business and finance courses, which added nothing
to my skill with women but overcame one of my perceived
weaknesses: a lack of qualifications on my CV.

I also fixed my fashion sense over a period of two years.
I went from wearing baggy jeans, Nike tops and trainers to
well-fitting, stylish designer clothes. I initially made
mistakes and bought terrible items (the fake Versace polo
shirt with a huge logo, the Zegna suit that was two sizes
too 'baggy'!), but over time I refined my style and learned
a lot about labels, design, fit and fabrics.

During this time, people started to regard me as
confident and women started paying me more attention
because of this – and also because of my improved sense of
style. But I was very focused on learning and stayed out of
the social scene. As a result, I didn't sleep with any women
between March 2003 and November 2005 – apart from a
couple of times with my ex-girlfriend!

In September 2005, I met a man called Tyler in Starbucks,

Leicester Square, central London. He was sitting around with a bunch of strange-looking guys; they were carrying papers with graphics about how to approach women. I listened in, but it didn't make much sense to me. I asked Tyler whether it was a speed-dating event they were preparing for, and he broke everything down for me. He told me to buy a book called *The Game* and explained what it was all about. I later found out that he was one of the most well-known 'pick-up artists', or PUAs, in the world. It was his job to teach men how to pick up women, and he spent all his time working out routines and openers – prepared lines to say to women, from conversation starters and little stories to games, tricks and gimmicks. He'd taken his name from Brad Pitt's character in *Fight Club*, the rebel against society and leader of like-minded men. A true alpha male.

From looking at these guys, I didn't really buy into the idea that they could have any success with women – they looked too geeky – but, nevertheless, I bought *The Game* as soon as it was published. It's the story of Neil Strauss, a journalist who was sent to infiltrate this underground society of pick-up artists. The book wasn't great in terms of usable techniques, but it was an introduction to a new world of possibility. After reading it, I looked up featured names like Mystery and David Deangelo and spent the next six months devouring all the material I could find on the subject in the form of ebooks, DVDs and audio courses only available from relatively obscure websites. Both Tyler and Deangelo were major influences: Deangelo is a more mainstream teacher of seduction, one of the few guys who (rather than seeming weird or geeky) I could imagine women being attracted to. He is naturally funny, very confident and knowledgeable. But the other guys seemed weird to me, and I couldn't understand how a woman would find them attractive once their tricks ran out. This was the start of my divergence from the established methods, and led to where I am now – a teacher of Natural Game.

I did less than ten approaches in those six months, but felt I had a good handle on the area as I had studied it as thoroughly as I had my business courses. Shortly after reading *The Game*, I went to Singapore on holiday. I was visiting my ex-girlfriend, who I still felt something for but was no longer in love with. She did, however, have a colleague that I was attracted to. I was there for a month and bumped into this girl a few times. She was educated in Oxford, and I loved her Liz Hurley accent. One night, when we were in a club and she was sitting next to me, I put a small amount of my learning to use. She put her hand on my leg, so I put my hand on her leg. She started rubbing my leg, so I did the same. She took my hand, so I leaned in and kissed her.

I would have been happy with just a kiss, this being the second girl I'd kissed in my life! However, she escalated things further; "Let's go," she said, and took me outside to a cab and back to my hotel. She did all the work. In the hotel room, she took her clothes off, lay back and made my job as easy as it could possibly be. I felt very good after this;

like a real man, I was finally getting somewhere! The sex on a one-night stand is never as good for me as it is with a girl I feel really connected with. But, as someone that felt very sexually inexperienced, there were certain things I needed to get checked off my to-do list!

My confidence was already boosted from all the pick-up artist theory in my head. I felt I had a secret weapon I could deploy with devastating results. And why not – it had a one hundred per cent success rate so far! Other guys didn't know this stuff. They were idiots! I was going to clean up! Okay, so she was the one who said, "Let's go," who got us in a cab and took us back to a hotel; she was a friend of a friend, rather than a cold approach – but hey! I'd got the result, and I'd be able to get it any time I wanted . . .

In March 2006, I moved to London. I picked the location specifically for meeting women, going out and being sociable – Leicester Square. I didn't know anyone, so I knew I'd be forced to get out there and meet people.

I had wanted to move to London for years. I was never happy living in Cambridge. I found it too small, the people too unfriendly and boring, and I didn't have the kind of social life that I wanted. Why did I wait so long? The answer may be the same thing that holds you back in many areas of your life; it was a *huge* realisation to know I was afraid that, if I moved to London and it was a failure, I'd be back in Cambridge *and* would no longer have the dream of something better to hold on to.

So at its core was fear of failure. Look at any big steps

that you've avoided taking and maybe it's for the same reason.

I didn't know anyone when I moved to London. My flatmates were cool and we got on, but they had no social circle so I didn't get to meet people that way. Eventually, I met some London pick-up artists via online forums and hooked up with them.

I went out with these guys and gave them the kind of respect I'd give the master PUAs described in *The Game*. I thought that anyone who had spent years working on something would be very good at it. However, I quickly found out that most of these guys could talk a good talk, but they didn't seem to be able to start conversations and hold women's interest, never mind close the deal. I'd see them approach and the girls would look at each other with a 'help me' face, or they'd smile politely, then shake their heads and say, "What was up with that guy?" after he turned his back. The guys would be very happy with their skills if they just managed a short conversation without being rejected. Luckily, I had better role models (on video and audio), but it did make me question their potential. If these guys had taken years of focused effort to get to this level, maybe I'd never be able to become what I wanted to be.

I had to ratchet down my expectations a little bit. I realised pretty quickly that my goal should not be to 'game' like a pick-up artist but like a natural, someone who exudes the qualities a woman will naturally be attracted to, who doesn't need tricks and gimmicks or lies to make women fall for him.

Over the next few weeks, I met some more of these guys. Most of them I didn't really want to hang out with, but I did meet two, Eugene and Conor, who were cool, and I tried to go out to clubs with them as often as possible. I was going out four nights a week. At this point I'd been to a club less than thirty times, and found the environment very uncomfortable. These nights would normally involve us opening twenty or so groups of girls, though few successfully.

I was overcoming my fear of talking to women, and a couple of times I had a nice conversation thanks to my pre-existing introvert skill of being a good listener. I think I could have become disillusioned at this point if I was purely focused on the end result. I might have come back home every night and complained, "Well, I didn't get any numbers again," but I managed to view every week as a successful advancement. At first it was, "Today, I achieved X number of approaches"; then it was, "Today, I had X number of good interactions." That way, I was able to stay positive in the early days.

I had a regular night out in Covent Garden with Conor, where I started to get some good results. We'd act as each other's 'wings', one of us would take care of the friends of our target girls so a strong connection and a number close could be made. We'd take it in turns and, by working together, we'd get much better results. I'd been out with other guys and it was something like a military operation; we'd split into teams and have a strategy for opening groups. I remember one night, when I went out with the pick-up guys from the forum, someone put us into groups and sent us out on a mission to approach ten women each with an opener he'd given us. This felt weird and unnatural, but would have been cool had there been results. But there weren't any; I never saw anyone get a number the whole time. With Conor, we had a fun vibe together and we tried to make it more natural and free-flowing. Even if we got nowhere, we'd have a fun time.

With a wing helping you, it's easy to avoid getting blown out. If the conversation flags, your girl sees her friend conversing with your pal and is forced to carry on chatting with you, instead of telling you she needs to go to the bathroom or the dance-floor. Working alone requires a lot more skill, because if you lose it for even a second she'll get bored and move on.

I was able to get a few number closes with Conor in various clubs, but nothing came of them. One girl I was sure I'd meet for a date (we had a great conversation, I took her number, we arranged to meet on a Wednesday at Salsa) texted me to say she hurt her ankle at the gym. After that, I tried to meet her a few times but it never happened. I don't know if the excuse was real or not, but these days this kind of thing just doesn't occur. I had no idea how to use physical contact (kino-escalation) to get a kiss close in the club, though by now I was pretty confident in interacting with women. The girls I was approaching were often hot, and they complimented me on my looks. This was new to me, and it felt good. I think several things had changed which increased my attractiveness: I was better dressed, with a better haircut and better body language, I'd removed a lot of my nervous tics and bad mannerisms, and – probably most importantly – I was radiating a new level of confidence. If you have high confidence and self-esteem, people will be more attracted to you than if you feel that you are a loser. I was projecting a more attractive energy.

The next big realisation happened about three weeks into my London adventure. I was in a Soho club with Conor and another guy when Conor approached two Swedish girls. I didn't act as his wing straight away because I was talking to an Australian girl. It didn't get far, so I went over to join the three of them. Conor was focused on his girl and mine was eighteen years old, Swedish and pretty cute. I was sitting there on the arm of her chair for *a full hour*, talking to her; eventually I told her to move up and, when she did, I sat down next to her and carried on talking.

I was getting no touching from her, and didn't know what the hell I should do. My one-night stand in Singapore only happened because she touched my leg first, and I just matched her kino-escalation and led with the kiss. Anyhow, I said to myself, "Fuck it," put my arm around her and went for the kiss. Lo and behold, it worked; she was into it. Now I know I probably could have done it after

15

thirty seconds, but the point was that it shifted something in my mind – you don't *need* to ask if it's okay to kiss. Women like men to lead; asking if she wants to kiss, or waiting ages to do it, is just unattractive. In this case I didn't have the knowledge I have now, so I could have been rejected when I went for it – but, if you don't try, you won't ever find out if it was on or not. (I should emphasise here that lunging in suddenly for a kiss is a terrible thing to do, and you should read the chapters later in this book to learn the way to do it smoothly.)

Conor left early because it didn't pan out with his girl. Reflecting on this episode, I realise it would have been easy to take my girl home. (Her friend was happy to leave her in my care!) I didn't, probably because I was buzzing from the kiss close and didn't imagine it was possible.

I was happy now in London; I had friends and felt like I was in control of things a little more. I had a lot of confidence and was on a high because I was able to attract women. I'd learned the basic structure of a seduction from six months of theory and a few weeks in the field. Admittedly, I spent way too long geeking out on the material, sitting in my house, thinking I was making progress, and putting off the challenging event – the thing that would really test me. Now I got much more out of the experience of going out and talking to women, and spent the next month refining my approach. We used a lot of 'canned material' (which I'll explain later) and it worked to help attract girls.

The next milestone happened one night in a Covent Garden club. My friend identified a hot girl. She was tall, blonde and slim, with blue eyes. These days she'd be of the usual standard, but at the time she was very hot. I think a natural consequence of increased ability and choice with women is an increased fussiness. I know women won't like this, but looks are something I can be very fussy about, they are important to me. From spending so much time with women you get desensitised to standard levels of beauty, and it takes something more special to catch the eye. You date a girl with a flat stomach and then you want that every time; you date a girl with beautiful eyes and you want that every time; you date a girl with a nice ass and you want that every time.

Anyway, I sat next to this babe and just chatted away. After some teasing banter to challenge her, I lightly touched her leg and arm and she reciprocated. I went for the kiss after about five minutes. Then I led her around the club – "Let's go get a drink. Let's dance. Let's sit down." We got quite hot and heavy, then I just got up, took her hand and said, "Let's go." She started walking with me, but asked, "Where?" I said, "Somewhere else," and walked her out of the club to my house. I let her sit on my bed (there was nowhere else to sit in my room!) and went to get some wine. When I came back we chatted and drank, and then I moved in for some more kissing. I took her glass and laid her down on the bed. I was lying on top and kissing her, but didn't really know how to escalate past that. My actions

17

weren't very decisive and it took me a long time to get her top off. If she wasn't completely up for it, I think I would have blown it by not taking the initiative. Maybe she thought it was nice to have such long foreplay! An hour later we were naked in the bed, and finally getting it on.

She left early in the morning to get back home, and I was buzzing. I'd met an attractive girl, and within a few hours had persuaded her I was good enough for her to sleep with me. I guess it's a form of validation. We have unconditional love from our family, and over time people can develop a fondness, but it's a nice compliment for a stranger to fall for us.

I thought she could become my girlfriend, but I met her for a date on another day and the attraction had vanished. I didn't like that she smoked; I didn't like her accent; I didn't like her shoes or the way she walked. We went to the cinema and she took her shoes off, then I smelled her feet. *Yuk!* We watched a scary film and she was sweating, with sweaty palms. Double *yuk!* After all these little things, I wasn't attracted to her any more, and she equally went off me. I felt like Jerry Seinfeld when he dumps the girl for silly reasons, but I didn't call her again and she didn't call me.

Over the next month or so, I got plenty of kisses and slept with a few more girls. I took about four salsa classes. I didn't pick up any girls in the class, because they were generally not up to standard – but I did devise my 'salsa escalation', where I go and ask the girl if she can salsa and then dance my way into a kiss.

During the same time, I was still studying the theory and going out to refine my technique. Bit by bit, I was gaining confidence and adding more skills to my repertoire. I kissed a Serbian chick in one minute with my salsa escalation; she was six feet tall, toned and tanned, blonde with blue eyes. It took seven hours before she slept with me, and then she was my girl for about a month.

During my time with the Serbian girl, I think I only kiss-closed one other girl, and that was when I trained with Brent (a renowned American pick-up artist). He came to the UK in May, and I decided that I'd either learn a lot from him or maybe make a resolution to become a trainer too. I paid $1000 plus expenses for one evening from 7pm to 2am. He was good looking, confident and cool, but the training was a letdown. He didn't demo anything cool. He couldn't entertain two girls after I engaged their cute friend (they quickly dragged her away). He only said I should talk louder and escalate faster. That was his only advice. Very nice guy though. Maybe my level was already high. Anyhow, I pulled a nice girl that night.

This was the first time I was disappointed with the skills of a well-known guru. There were many more to come over the next few months! Now, when I meet famous pick-up gurus, my attitude is: "Hey, if they are great I'll learn something – and if they aren't it'll make me more confident." Win-win!

Over the next few months I improved my game, gained more confidence, had more hot girls and met various influential characters – most importantly Steve Jabba and Anthony P, who were introduced to me in a bar by one of the weird guys I hung out with when I first moved to London. These two were naturals who had found out about the pick-up arts after they were already successful with women. We went out a lot and gamed together.

In June, I had started Puatraining.com and began by doing one-on-ones. I was a skilled teacher, could communicate clearly and was able to analyse a person's strengths and weaknesses very quickly to give them practical advice. Through teaching, I perfected my stuff and was forced to game way more tightly. I learned how to control my state, instead of only being able to game when I felt like it.

In July, I went travelling through eleven countries for two months with my friend Steve. During this holiday, my skills in kino, non-verbal pick-up, dance-floor game and other areas all got a huge boost. I came back comfortable and confident in nightclubs. Steve is a legend, and few people have seen his skills when he is at the top of his game. I saw him do things on holiday that gave me the shivers! It was next-level game.

Fast forward to today. I am going to parties with celebrities to learn how to game in that environment. I'm working with the guys at PUAtraining.com to further refine the system. And I'm travelling to different countries to test my game internationally. How do I pick up girls now? I have a routine stack that can be successful every day of the week, one that uses an unbreakable opener followed by calculated responses, built-in emotional spikes, seductive language patterns and a host of psychological tricks. But you know what? *I don't use this stuff!* I want to be able to game naturally. I don't want to know what I'm going to say next. I like to test my intelligence and exercise my mental muscles. I want to make a better self, instead of constructing a character that I can step in and out of.

Success? I'm now completely satisfied with my love life. I meet very high-value girls who are in the top 0.1 per cent of the population in terms of their desirability, and I feel like, if I'm ever single, I'll be able to find a girlfriend without too much trouble. Put simply, I now have *choice* with women. I prefer a real relationship to a casual one, but this is what choice means – I will only be single when I want to; I will have the kind of women I want in my life and won't have to settle for someone that isn't quite right for me. Mainly, it means I won't ever lie in bed at night wondering if I'll ever get a date!

The Science of Attraction

WHAT IS IT THAT A WOMAN ACTUALLY LOOKS FOR IN A MAN? WHAT ARE THE ELEMENTS THAT MAKE *HIM* THE ONE SHE WANTS, RATHER THAN ALL THE OTHER MEN?

Looks: Men vs. Women

Lots of men think they need to be very good looking in order to get more women. That is because looks are a major consideration for men. Beautiful women require a man that is 'good looking enough', someone that isn't objectionable, but they don't have to be gorgeous. In fact, so many women have told me that it is better if the guy is not super-handsome, because it means he is less likely to cheat or to look for someone better. She wants to be the best-looking one in the relationship! Over time, a woman will find your physical imperfections 'cute' and, as she falls more in love with you, her attraction to your particular looks will grow. If you are an average-looking man reading this, then yes, you *can* have a beautiful woman who is attracted to you.

Sometimes a girl will tell me that one of my friends who is great with women is handsome. Technically, he usually isn't. What she is actually saying is that she is attracted to this man, and she *assumes* it is because he is handsome. In fact, she is attracted to his other qualities:

- His alpha maleness.
- His unflappability.
- His powerful frame.
- His leadership.
- His sexual confidence.
- His calmness.

I've gone out with students who have got bad reactions, and girls have found them unattractive. After some work on their confidence, and after they have achieved some success, the same girls are saying, "Wow, he looks really good!" and wondering if he has new clothes, has been working out or has whitened his teeth. In reality he has done none of this, but is projecting a new self-image. If you have no self-belief, if you think you are useless, you project an ugly self-image. If you think you are the main man, you project an attractive self-image and actually become more attractive. I've seen this in hundreds of students, and it has made me realise that a huge element of attractiveness stems from your state of mind.

Attraction Process: Men vs. Women

If you had one hundred men in a room and a beautiful woman came in, how many of those men would sleep with her right there and then based on her looks? I'd estimate around ninety per cent. If you reverse the situation, with one hundred women in a room as an attractive man comes in, how many would sleep with him right there and then? I'm thinking twenty per cent or less.

Men make a huge commitment to the woman before they have even spoken to her, based solely on her looks. They would commit to buying a girl a drink, spending the night with her, buying her dinner, going away for the weekend with her, and maybe more – all based solely on her looks. Because of this, it means that when we see an attractive woman we come in *too hot*, we show her that she can't do much wrong, that we've already made our mind up. That is why women say that men are only after one thing, it's because they have seen the way men look at them as they approach. They put on a smile, and the man has already made up his mind that he wants her. She can't 'lose' him during the conversation, he's still going to ask for her number. If a man gets a girlfriend, generally he loses attraction after a certain point and is drawn to other women, especially those with the opposite physical looks or character to the one he is with. If he is with a brunette, he will check out blondes more.

A woman's attraction process is different; she becomes more attracted to a man over time. His imperfections become cute, she gets comfortable with him and his looks become the standard against which she measures what she likes. If you ask a girl to describe what she admires in terms of looks, she'll often describe the last man she was really fond of. I'll meet girls who will tell me that I'm not their type, but give it some time and they start describing me as their ideal man and regarding men in the street as attractive because they look like me. The woman's attraction process is why most relationships happen via the social circle (see below).

PROBLEMS WITH RELATIONSHIPS – MEN VS. WOMEN

The number of people who are unsatisfied with their love lives is high. We know lots of single people and lots in relationships they aren't completely happy with. It is rare if we have within our social circle one example of a truly solid relationship.

This book is for helping men to become better; the reason it can't be for both sexes is because men and women have their problems at different stages of male–female interaction. A man's most common failing is that he can't even pluck up the courage to start a conversation, and, if he can, he finds it difficult to evolve that to a date, and eventually to a relationship. Even if he is very attractive, he won't get approached very often at all. The man is still expected to make the first moves, to start the conversation, to ask for the woman's number, to ask her for a date, to go for the kiss, etc. There is much more of a requirement for him to be active in starting the relationship.

An attractive woman can go to a busy nightspot, and she is almost guaranteed to be approached over and over again. All she has to do is decide if she will talk to the guy, if she will give her number, if she will meet for a date, and if she wants to let the guy kiss her. In most cases, the man has decided that he wants her before he has spoken to her, and there is not much she can say or do to make him change his mind. She doesn't need to be funny, confident or fascinating.

But it's not all easy for a woman. Her problem comes later in separating the good guys from the bad guys. Her logical mind wants a nice guy who is reliable, who she can introduce to her parents and who will always be there. However, her emotional mind wants to tame the wild guy, to meet someone who is unpredictable and surprising, someone she has to work for, that she could lose at any moment.

The nice guy usually gets dumped and the bad guy normally breaks a lot of hearts. For a while I thought I'd need to become 'the jerk that women love', and be an asshole in order to get more women and avoid having girls dump me – but then I realised it's actually possible to stay a nice guy while introducing some of the characteristics of the bad guy, without actually being bad. (See the subsection on 'Frame of Mind in a Relationship'.)

This is the way society works at the moment. But, although this book is for men, I hope it will help women indirectly.

HOW MOST PEOPLE GET TOGETHER – SOCIAL CIRCLE

Most people in relationships have got together through their social circle. They worked together, went to school together or at least are friends of friends. It's a powerful factor when you meet someone who is part of your social circle (even if we loosely define 'social circle' as having an acquaintance in common):

- They know you are not an axe murderer.
- You can immediately add the friend-in-common's value to your own – the years she has known them, how much she likes them, etc.
- Comfort is built in – all that is required is attraction.
- You can work the seduction over a longer period of time.
- Your mutual friends will usually help get you together.

This is why it's easier to chat up women at a birthday party as opposed to a bar. At the party, even if you don't know the woman but approach her with, "How do you know Bob?" there is some element of trust, and also some obligation for social courtesy, which helps smooth an interaction.

Safety (from being a part of your group) and exposure to

the person over a long period of time are two powerful factors. It's not really a matter of choice, or real desire, but of convenience – almost settling for something. It can still be good, but if everyone felt they had complete choice they'd make much better decisions.

HOW TO HAVE COMPLETE CHOICE – THE HARDEST SKILL: THE COLD APPROACH

This is what this book is all about. You will see benefits to all your social interactions, but the skill of someone who is amazing with women is the ability to progress an interaction with a stranger all the way. You might have women you like in your social circle – but how much do you really like them, how much of their attraction is due to the time you have spent with them, and how attainable they are? Complete choice with women means we can get any woman we want. It means that if we see a girl in Starbucks we can approach her, and if the situation is right we can have some kind of relationship with her. It means we don't just see the women we work with, or friends of friends, as potential partners, but the women in bars, clubs, supermarkets, even in a women's clothes shop or walking down the street.

Are Johnny Depp and Brad Pitt amazing with women? They might not be! They are in a position where they have everyone in their social circle, so they are never going to be treated like an anonymous stranger. They also have an incredibly high status and social value. But there is a rumour that Brad Pitt was terrible with women when he first moved to Hollywood. The man who is best with women is not a celebrity – a celebrity can be lazy and still get all the women he wants. The best in the world is a man who no one knows, who can approach a woman in any situation and get whatever he wants from that situation. People can buy a model agency, or engineer a life which guarantees hot women – think Peter Stringfellow and Hugh Hefner – but wouldn't it be better to be able to get these girls without social advantages, without any promise of their working for you, when they are attracted to *you* and *your* qualities rather than what you can offer?

Pre-Game

YOUR FIRST IMPRESSION –
PAVING THE WAY

A WOMAN'S FIRST IMPRESSION OF YOU IS NOT FORMED WHEN YOU FIRST OPEN YOUR MOUTH TO SPEAK TO HER: IT'S FORMED WHEN SHE FIRST CATCHES A GLIMPSE OF YOU OUT OF THE CORNER OF HER EYE.

A few years ago, a woman would have been able to tell I was insecure, unhappy, unconfident, unfashionable, low-energy, unsociable, non-sexual and shy just from looking at me. Why would she want to talk to me? How would she feel if I approached her?

I guess I knew this, and that is why I didn't even bother trying to talk to girls. But it's frustrating; you know you are a nice guy, nicer than the guy she is with, nicer than your friends who are in relationships. You know you'd be good for her, but she isn't in the slightest bit interested.

30

The good news is that you can retain your good qualities, learn some new things, and become a man that naturally attracts women.

It's difficult to know how you look to others, because you don't have a video camera following you around all the time. However, we can work to make the best possible first impression by being aware of the necessary components. There are various elements that affect a woman's initial perception of you:

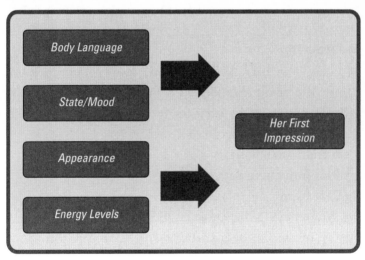

I'll go through each of these and break down into easy-to-follow steps how you can make the improvements that allow a great first impression. Most of the examples will be based on being in bars, pubs or clubs, since these are where most people socialise, and also where the mistakes that guys make are most obviously on display.

PRE-OPENING BODY LANGUAGE: STANDING OUT POSITIVELY

When I did go to bars and clubs, I remember that I felt very uncomfortable just standing around; I'd need to go and get a drink, nervously sip it, walk around a bit, go to the toilet, get another drink. I was never relaxed in that environment. Now when I'm in a club, I'm as comfortable as if I were in my house. It is a process of desensitisation, and also of being aware of how you look at all times, whilst having some techniques to fake it until you make it.

The Wrong Way

Most guys in bars and clubs don't look happy; they get drinks and stand shoulder to shoulder, checking out the girls. This immediately creates a negative first impression. They see a guy that is:

- On the pull.
- Not interesting to his friend.
- Not happy.
- Not enjoying the music or the atmosphere.
- On his way to being drunk.

Of course, these guys are doing one thing right – they are out of their house! I was literally *scared* of being in a club, even if I wasn't approaching any girls. Getting comfortable in the environment is step one for anyone. I remember one of my customers who couldn't hold eye contact, felt people were laughing at him and had all kinds of self-esteem issues. The first two times we went out, we just hung out in a club to get him comfortable in the environment. That's always got to be the first step.

The right way: alpha-male body language

So how do you stand out positively from all the other guys in a bar/club? The first thing to do is to look like you're having fun and are happy to be there. When you're with your friends, face them and engage them. If you're standing face to face, you can each cover one hundred and eighty degrees of the location and check out all the girls you want, over each other's shoulders. Women are subtle, and this is what they usually do. When I started going out in London to meet women, I saw a huge difference in the success and attention we got depending on how much I enjoyed the other guy's company. When I had fun with my friend and it showed, women were more attracted to us. A woman looks at a guy having a good time and, on some level, wants to be part of the fun. When we were simply out looking for women, Terminator-style, we didn't get this positive attention. Your mood will also affect your results; you will do much better when you feel good and are having fun.

If you must walk around trying to find the hot girls, do the "Where's Bob?" face and look as if you're looking for someone. This subtle difference allows you to check out everyone in the whole place without having the pick-up-guy vibe. Something funny happens to me sometimes: I actually get more attention from doing "Where's Bob?",

33

because, if I'm doing it whilst standing next to very hot girls, they wonder why I'm *not* looking at them.

When you're speaking, facial animation and gestures draw attention and make it look like you're having fun. Someone who seems like a fun-loving, sociable guy is someone a woman wants to speak to. Someone who is not having much fun with their friends, and only wants to check women out, will not get a good reaction when he approaches. I never used to find gesturing or moving around natural, but now it is. When you incorporate a new form of behaviour, it will feel unnatural at first. A good way to feel comfortable in gesturing is to bend your arms at the elbows and clasp your hands in front of you when you are talking. Throw out the occasional gesture from this position and it will become a habit in no time. Get your hands out of your pockets, and make sure the gesture doesn't come from your side – which is just weird! People who naturally gesture can easily work in some casual touching – the upper arm, back, etc. People that have barely any movement in them will find it hard to touch the woman in conversation. Most guys stand there fidgeting, shifting their weight, moving their feet, moving their hands, nervously taking sips of their drink. To stand out from all these guys, incorporate the following alpha-male behaviour:

Legs: Stand with your feet slightly wider apart than is natural. It will feel strange at first but you'll also feel completely rooted, like a tree. You'll no longer constantly change position or shift your weight.

Arms: Most people I train have a problem with fidgeting;

they move their hands around, play with things, put their hands in their pockets and just can't stay still. This is a sign of a lack of confidence, and women will pick up on this immediately. Here's a trick to get over this: put your thumb against your index and middle fingers and let your hands fall to your sides. This removes the natural tendency for the fingers to find something to do. You can stay in this position comfortably for hours without moving. Importantly, don't touch your face.

Eyes: Don't look down! It conveys weakness. Be confident, hold eye contact with people. But remember, it isn't a staring match; soft, natural eye contact is what you need.

Head: Move your head slowly, it conveys high status. Quick head movements make you look nervous.

Space: Take up lots of space. When sitting, spread yourself out. When standing, have a wide, confident stance or use gestures. When dancing, move around the dance-floor a lot and use big arm movements (though be careful not to knock people over). In the past, I always used to get barged out of the way and my toes trodden on; since I started using alpha body language, people give me more space and this never happens. You'll know you are doing things right when the same happens to you.

MISSION ONE

Practise the alpha stance in your house, see how it looks in the mirror. Next time you're in a bar, observe other people's body language based on the rules above. See who has good and bad body language. Be very aware of your own and try to click into the alpha body-language mode.

Review

Your first impression is very important, and because so many guys create a bad first impression it is easy to stand out in a positive way. Breaking old habits is a process of first becoming aware of what you are doing wrong, then noticing when you are doing it, stopping it and eventually replacing this behaviour. If I train someone I can tell them all the things that no one else will ever tell them about their nervous tics, their ugly mannerisms, the things that negatively affect their first impression. I used to laugh nervously and touch my face, and it took my brutally honest cousin to point this out.

I often videotape students to show them how they look; it's usually a big surprise. A good way to become aware, if you don't have someone who will be completely honest, is to see how your behaviour looks in other people. Watch guys talking to girls, watch guys standing in the bar; see who looks cool and who doesn't, who looks needy and who doesn't. Notice other people doing things you do, and see how they look.

EVOLUTION OF A NATURAL: MARCH 2006

When I first moved to London and started going out, I was forcing myself to do as many approaches a night as possible.

I would do as many as twenty in a few hours. It gave me a buzz to be talking to so many attractive women that I'd never met before. I must have talked to more women in just a few weeks than I had in my entire life. I love female energy and being in the company of pretty women, so I was happy just to have these short interactions.

I believe it is necessary to do lots of approaches at first. Looking back, this was very useful for me. You need to desensitise yourself and remove approach anxiety, but, more than that, you need to get out of your own head and get focused on the other person. When we are thinking a lot about our own body language, our voice, what we are saying, what we are going to do next, we can't focus enough on the other person to read signals and give them what they want.

During my first thirty or so approaches, I'd be talking to a girl but most of my attention would be focused on what to say next, how my body language was, whether my voice was loud enough, my sweaty palms, and I'd miss all the little signals that she was giving me. I remember approaching two girls in a coffee shop; I saw that they had a tube map and, without thinking much, I approached and asked if I could look at it to see how to get to Earl's Court. I asked them where they were from; they were Czech and studying English in London; I was laughing nervously and blushed, but I was getting a positive reaction. I did something I'd never done before here, talking for what seemed like minutes (but was probably not more than twenty seconds) about how I went to Seville and got the teaching English qualification. This was the first time I'd had serious attention from a group of girls focused on me for more than a few seconds. It was a real breakthrough, because prior to this I'd just asked questions to avoid having the attention focused on me. I still messed up though; I asked what they were doing later, they said they had to meet a friend soon, and I said, "Oh okay, bye then." I took what they said in the worst possible way, and sat back down. When they were leaving, they hung around expectantly but I didn't have the courage to 're-open' and ask for the number. A common mistake guys make is hitting the self-destruct button: they take the tiniest potentially negative thing as an excuse to run away.

So here I was, going out and approaching twenty girls a night. I'd have some fear about it but I'd force myself.

(As a side-note, you might wonder why I didn't spend hundreds of pounds if I was going out so much. The answer is that, in those early days, I never touched a drop of alcohol. I'd go to clubs and bars where we could get in free, and I'd only drink tap water. If I'd drunk the average amount every time I'd gone out, it would have cost me thousands of pounds by now, and if I'd offered to buy every girl I talked to a drink – well, let's just say I would have had to sell the laptop I'm writing this book on, and you'd never be reading this.)

MODELLING ON ACTORS: LEARNING FROM THE BEST

Hollywood actors are not natural. They have calculated poses, body language and voices. Look at the faces they pull

38

in pictures and in films; they are not poses that normal people assume. That's because they are manipulating their facial muscles in particular ways: Tom Cruise's smile, Brad Pitt's eyes, Colin Farrell's sexual bad-boy look, George Clooney's voice, are all manufactured. You can model a look based on celebrities that stands out as much as theirs does.

I imitated the looks I saw in films and magazines in front of the mirror. Some people might find that embarrassing, but, believe me, Hollywood actors have done the same thing. I felt like an idiot watching *The Last Samurai*, *Meet Joe Black* and *24* in front of the mirror, copying their facial expressions, but that feeling went away the first time a girl said I looked like a model! Models have calculated poses, so, if you work on your poses just like they have, you will look more like a model!

Knowing how you look at all times, and manipulating your look to achieve particular effects, is very powerful. Knowing how to turn on a sexy and seductive look at the right time will make a girl melt. So don't copy Mr Bean, choose a man with broad appeal!

BODY LANGUAGE

There are two ways to make a cold approach. One is the cold walk-up where you directly approach a girl and engage her. The second is a more casual, seemingly spontaneous way to open: your target is a step or two away, and you casually turn around, or step over, and open. In both instances, there are steps you can take to create a favourable first impression.

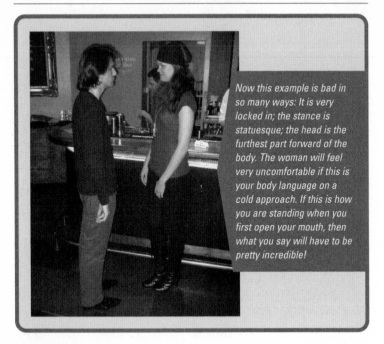

Now this example is bad in so many ways: It is very locked in; the stance is statuesque; the head is the furthest part forward of the body. The woman will feel very uncomfortable if this is your body language on a cold approach. If this is how you are standing when you first open your mouth, then what you say will have to be pretty incredible!

Bad Body Language

Most men walk up and get in the girl's face. Do this to someone you know and it's bad enough. Ask someone to do this to you to see how it feels. It creates a reflex response of wanting to step back and put your hands up. This is putting a lot of pressure on an interaction before it has even begun. Unless the girl is obviously interested in you, it's a bad move. This type of face-to-face interaction also feels like it could go on forever. Both people look locked in, and the only way for the interaction to end is if someone turns one hundred and eighty degrees. In the event of a blow-out, everyone around you has seen what

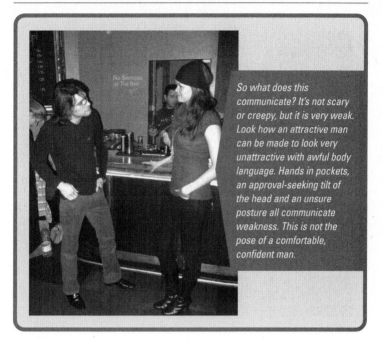

So what does this communicate? It's not scary or creepy, but it is very weak. Look how an attractive man can be made to look very unattractive with awful body language. Hands in pockets, an approval-seeking tilt of the head and an unsure posture all communicate weakness. This is not the pose of a comfortable, confident man.

has happened so you're putting even more pressure on yourself. Once you understand body language and can read women's reactions, you will see how bad at this most men are. This is the kind of knowledge that will boost confidence, because you will know that you know how to do things better than other men.

Good body language

Here's what you do when opening: your feet should be pointing away from the target and only your face should be pointing towards her. By doing this, you can comfortably get close enough to kino, but the interaction

Here we have a better posture; it's open and more confident. There is eye contact, but it is lessened by the head being in line with the body and by the use of gestures. One foot is pointing away, which makes it feel less locked in and more casual.

The low-pressure way to open is with the feet pointing away from the target and only the face pointing towards. This looks very impermanent and is very comfortable for the girl. It also seems more spontaneous.

isn't as locked in and you aren't invading her personal space. To eject from the group, you'd just have to turn your head and not face her any more. I think most people respond well to being opened this way, because they have had many short, innocent interactions like this with people who are on their way to somewhere.

Approaching a seated group

When you approach a seated group, you want to quickly get down to the same level as the target. It's very difficult to close when you're standing over them.

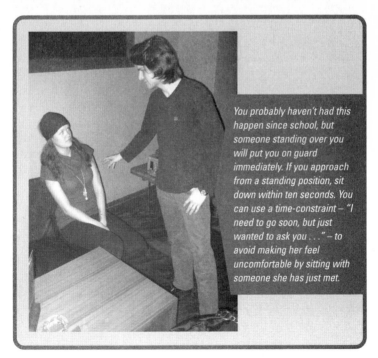

You probably haven't had this happen since school, but someone standing over you will put you on guard immediately. If you approach from a standing position, sit down within ten seconds. You can use a time-constraint – "I need to go soon, but just wanted to ask you . . ." – to avoid making her feel uncomfortable by sitting with someone she has just met.

If there are no spare chairs, or you would need to ask her to move to make space for you, you should start off in a position like this so that you are on her level. But don't stay like this for too long as it becomes weird. Quickly ask her to move over, or sit on the arm of the chair, or even share her chair with her.

This is the essence of indirect body language. Direct game (showing interest straight away) obviously requires that you put more pressure on an interaction earlier on, so making the girl feel comfortable and minimising your chances of getting rejected are not so much of an issue. Direct body language is all about presenting a sexual vibe, touching quickly and escalating sexually.

EVOLUTION OF A NATURAL: APRIL 2006

I was going out a lot, generally starting conversations, running out of things to say and then making fast excuses to leave. Sometimes I'd get into a long conversation, which was nice, but I wouldn't direct it properly either. I remember when I went out with some guys to a bar in Chinatown which at the time was called Bar Room Bar. I approached a girl with an opinion opener and we got into a nice chat. She studied psychology, so we had a common interest. I didn't need to make any excuse to leave, so I'd got over a sticking point but then encountered a new one: I was in a nice conversation and found the girl attractive, but I felt uncomfortable going for the number. I felt like it would be a betrayal, so I just said it was nice to talk to her and I left. The reason I was getting into these situations was that I was too nice, I cared about what people thought about me, and I hadn't expressed any interest – so it wouldn't flow naturally to then ask for her number. Since I was never going to see her again, I might as well have asked, but – because I was using such an indirect method to talk to her, and trying not to compliment her or show interest (in case it seemed needy or weak) – it would have seemed unnatural.

I'd been going out for a few weeks, and what I'd managed to do was get myself to the point where I wasn't too scared about approaching, and where I could generally get into a good conversation. My sticking point was escalating things so that I could either get a date out of it, or physically escalate things to a kiss. I still felt good, because just interacting with women was an exciting new thing, and I could see that I'd already made a lot of progress. My first kiss came with the Swedish girl in the Soho club, and from that point I became bolder and started working the interaction towards the kiss, and towards sex.

FASHION

Women notice your appearance. They judge it instantly and, unlike your friends, they can tell if something doesn't match, is out of place or is just plain ugly. Good fashion advice is difficult to find, and most guys don't feel a need to concentrate on this area. I used to wear sports clothes, baggy jeans and clothing that never got complimented. I dressed for guys, not for girls, I wore what my friends at school would think was cool. I was comfortable, sure, but I didn't convey positivity through my dress. I got my first compliments about my clothes when I switched from trainers to shoes, bought a suede jacket and ditched the sportswear.

A fashion makeover takes a long time if you are getting everything wrong, and it isn't as simple as buying a new pair of shoes. The shoes won't work with your existing trousers and top, so you'll need new ones, and then your jacket will look strange, etc. A few simple rules will make a huge difference:

1. Don't dress generically

If your clothes are so plain that they couldn't be commented on by a woman, even if she was trying hard to find something to say, then you're generic. If you're wearing drab colours with standard cuts, and generally blend into the background, you're not making the most of personal style. Look around at other men and see how much you can say about their dress sense. If their jeans have details and funky touches, they are better than standard Levis. If the shirt or T-shirt has a tailored cut, a slogan, cool detailing, funky colours or a picture, it's something outside of the generic and reflects your personality in a better way.

2. Spend money on the right things

An expensive shirt or jeans are wasted if your shoes are ugly. Spend a lot of money on a couple of good pairs of shoes (one black, one brown). You can mix cheap jeans and shirts with great shoes and it will make you look like you're wearing an expensive outfit. After nice shoes, the jacket is the second most important thing (in winter). Next is the shirt or T-shirt, and last are the jeans or trousers. A few great outfits are better than lots of average ones.

3. Match clothes correctly

Blue jeans and brown shoes is a better combination than blue and black. Don't wear more than three colours. Skinny trousers with a baggy jumper is wrong, the fits should all match. More than one bold colour probably means a clash. Sports shoes have no place, but designer trainers are okay.

4. Accessorise

A funky bracelet is worth more in terms of female attention than a $15,000 solid white gold watch. Find accessories like rings, bracelets and necklaces that work for you.

5. Get the best haircut possible

If you're not getting comments on your haircut, it could be better. Go to an expensive salon for a free consultation, find out what would be the best cut for your face shape and hair type, and then get it done in a cheaper place!

6. Look like you are successful with women

Unbutton your top buttons. Look around and copy sexual styles. Looking like you're successful with women is something you can't do with generic clothes. Think Colin Farrell.

PEACOCKING GONE WRONG

Peacocking is the technique of wearing clothes and accessories, or just generally adopting a style, that attract attention. There is a right and a wrong way to do it. Many wannabe ladies' men will copy the clothes and accessories of guys that are famously good with women, rock stars that have unique styles, etc. I see these guys around, and the problem with them is that they look incongruent – like they are wearing something because they *think* they should wear it. It doesn't suit them; it's not a style that represents their character. These guys will get attention, but subconsciously the woman will find it strange. They look weird and stand out in a bad way. If you peacock, wear things that you would like to wear because you think it works for *your* personality.

One night I wore a cowboy hat to China White, which is one of London's famous posh clubs. It was very effective! Compared to a normal night where no girl would come and talk to me, I had five or more girls coming up to me, taking my hat, trying it on, complimenting it. One girl who was a model tried it on, we got chatting, and at the end of it I got her number. I probably wouldn't have had the guts at the time to approach a girl like that. I'd love to say the story ended well, but I called her, didn't manage to arrange a date, then lost the phone along with her number! When you start getting lots of numbers, remember this rule: back them up!

STATE CONTROL: BEING 'IN THE ZONE' ANY TIME

'State' is how you feel at any particular moment. Everyone has had times when they feel 'in the zone', and times when they feel useless. State control is about trying to take the 'in the zone' feeling and generating it at will. It's something I didn't learn until I started training other men. Prior to that, my own state fluctuated based on the vibe of a place, my mood that day, my friends' mood, the quality of the girls around and my first interactions. When I started training people one-on-one and spending up to twelve hours focused on one person, I needed to always be 'on', not sometimes in state and sometimes not. I developed a system for getting myself into state consistently and on-demand. Neuro-linguistic programming teaches anchoring, which is basically a method of linking a state to a body movement. I took things a step further because anchoring wasn't enough for me. Here is my proven system forgetting into state:

I have affirmations (I'll explain these in more detail later), which I read to myself. At the same time, I play music that has very positive associations for me and gets me pumped up; I click my fingers and move my body to generate energy. After doing this a number of times, each thing is associated with the others. Before I train I do all three, but, while I'm out, the music, the finger-clicking or the affirmations alone will be enough to get me in state.

When I'm in state, I feel completely confident, able to approach anybody. I feel like the most attractive and powerful person in any situation. This belief means that I am able to blow groups of girls wide open at will. I am able to generate high energy for high-energy groups of girls, but can obviously calibrate and tone it down for low-energy groups. In the past, high-energy groups would intimidate me, so I'd only approach lower-energy groups.

In the early days of training, if I didn't have a connection with the student whilst teaching and I felt tired, my interactions might not go as well. Now I can sense when my state isn't good enough, and generate it instantly.

State control tools:
- Small MP3 player for taking your music (and recorded affirmations) anywhere.
- A sheet of paper with affirmations.
- Associate a body movement.

My state control was put to the test by a one-on-one customer. We'd set up weekly meetings of three hours each time. The first time, I got to know him and taught him some theory. The second time, I took him out and demoed, did lots of approaches, got some numbers and impressed him. The third time I took him out, he said that he was going to do all the work and that I could observe, feedback and adjust him. That was great, because that night I was tired and not up to doing any gaming myself. When I met him, he told me he felt tired and off-form, so he wanted *me* to open some girls. He even pointed out a table of five girls and said, "There you go." I was completely unprepared and not in the mood; I didn't have the energy to hold the attention of five women, so I snapped my fingers, got in state and, three seconds later, walked over with enough energy to hold their attention completely.

I open them with an opinion opener (life coaching,

see 'Openers' section). He doesn't come in and help, instead he just stands there watching, leaving me to do the hard work. For ten minutes I hold their attention; it's like spinning plates, constantly watching who is losing interest and bringing them back in by directing energy or conversation their way. Finally, they ask me who I'm with and I call him over; we each take a girl and the others talk amongst themselves. If I didn't have state control, those girls would have much rather carried on their conversation than listened to some low-energy, uninterested, tired guy.

Relaxed state control

I also have a relaxed state. This is very similar to the above, except I have associated a body and hand position (from Pranayama, which is a branch of yoga dedicated to breathing) to a state of mind, with very relaxing classical music or self-hypnosis audio. Now just the hand position on its own is enough to relax me, or even lower my heart rate. Pranayama yoga is one of the coolest things I've done; anyone who would like to be more relaxed and peaceful should check it out. When I did my first lesson I could hold my breath for one minute and forty-five seconds, which is about a minute more than usual, just by being so relaxed and using my lungs properly. I use the relaxed state to calm myself before any kind of stressful event, and then snap into the high-energy, confident state a few minutes before it's time for action.

MISSION TWO

Write some affirmations (check 'Inner Game' subsection on affirmations); collect all the music tracks that get you pumped up in one place. Play the music, read the affirmations out loud and associate a body movement. Do this before you go out. Do it just ten times and you should notice you are able to snap into this state when you are out.

EVOLUTION OF A NATURAL: MAY 2006

In May, I did a few courses. First I did an NLP Master Practitioner course. Put simply, it was £2250 down the drain. The interesting and useful content could have been condensed down to about half a day's worth of seminar. There was no refund policy, which is something I think should always make people wary. I learned a few small things, but the money and time could have been better spent. Still, the title NLP Master Practitioner *sounds* cool. The course was filled with happy–clappy people for whom everything was always fantastic, who interpreted every communication to a minute degree, making it impossible to have a normal conversation, and were very outwardly confident without really having anything to be confident about. My thoughts about most of the other attendees were summed up when, at one point, I was slumping in my chair when the filler guy was doing his bit, and the man next to me told me to sit up and pay attention because my "negative physiology" was affecting his mood. I said, "I've paid the same as you and I'll sit however I want; tell this guy to be more interesting."

May was a month of courses and personal development for me, because I'd also booked some training with Brent from America. I'd watched him on a DVD series and he had a fantastic reputation as one of the world's best naturals. He's famous for never taking a woman's number; he gives them his and is so cool that he expects them to chase him. I liked the sound of him, but after my experience with the NLP course I was a bit wary and wondered whether it would be up to scratch. Before he came, I found a way to make the situation win–win. If it was great training, I'd learn a lot; if it wasn't (and this guy charged $5000 for a weekend), then it meant that *I* could do it too.

We met at seven and chatted about general stuff – the weather, what he thought of London – and I waited for my real training to begin. We took a cab and I told him my background, waiting for the real training to begin. We ate an £80 dinner and he told me a bunch of stories about how cool he and his friends were, what they've done with women, and I waited for the real training to begin . . . Finally he said it was time to get to work and chat up some girls, but he said it should be very natural. He talked to a man and woman for a few minutes, very surface-level banter, no attraction, no special techniques – in fact, it was mundane, almost boring. I pointed out a hot girl, but he said we should just let things happen naturally rather than directly approaching someone. Later I realised that someone who is truly great can make something happen in any situation. When someone can *force* a situation and a result, instead of just waiting for something to happen to them, that is when they have real power and choice.

We later went to a nightclub; he was very big on noticing every little thing and telling me how cool it was – some girl looked at him (because his energy is good); the bouncer smiled and let us in the club (because he is the fun-loving, sociable guy), *but* what he missed was technique, the steps necessary to break down a method that would work for anyone in a learnable form. I expected feedback on my body language, conversation, eye contact, etc, etc. I got two pieces of feedback for my $1,500; they were: 1. Talk louder. 2. Escalate faster.

That was it. At the time it was disappointing, now it is shocking. I can look back and see what I would have told myself; I can watch a customer interact with a woman and list twenty things in twenty minutes that they were probably not aware of, but that will make a huge difference to their success. The fact is that it's too easy for people to build up reputations using online forum bragging, website hype, puff pieces in the press, etc. In this case my expectations were high, but they weren't even close to being met. Rather than thinking I was worth whatever the market would bear, I decided I'd start by charging £195, offer a refund policy, work as hard as I could for my customers, and charge more when I knew I deserved it.

ENERGY LEVELS AND HOLDING ATTENTION

Your energy levels are a tool you can use to better manage the reaction you get. You should be aware of the energy levels in a location, and also those of the groups you're going to open. You should aim to stand out in terms of your energy level. If you are somewhere where all the men are trying to look cool, then you would be better served by standing out as the fun-loving, sociable guy. If you're in a very high-energy environment, you should be the James Bond guy that moves slowly and smoothly and stands out in that way.

Look around a location and see the energy of the various groups. As a rule, you should aim to come in with higher energy than the group you're approaching. You need to be more interesting than what they were doing before you showed up, to maximise your chances of connecting.

This is an area where many guys have problems. Natural extroverts and good storytellers share an ability to hold the attention of a whole group. I've seen guys with nothing to say command attention just by looking interesting, and very interesting guys get blown out because they can't hold the group's attention. This was a big problem for me initially because of my naturally quiet and shy nature. However, it's a necessary skill in pick-up. When you're interrupting people you need to be interesting. The words you use are only a small part of that. The statistic that only seven per cent of communication is verbal is more relevant here than anywhere else. How do you learn to be more interesting? I've broken down the core components. As a natural introvert with none of these skills, I've been able to apply them effectively, and you can do the same.

So what are the actual elements that affect your energy levels?

• Gestures

Use hand gestures; they are necessary to hold the attention of larger groups. If you get used to gesturing, you'll find it easier to progress to touching and it'll seem more natural to the girl. At first, gesturing feels forced when you're not used to it, but it quickly becomes second nature. To get used to gesturing, bend your arms at the elbow and clasp your hands. Make this your new default position when in-set, and put gestures out from this position. A gesture or touch coming from hands by the side always looks strange – see the difference in other people.

• Voice-tone variation

Another aspect that adds interest and draws people's attention. Listen to broadcasters: you don't need to go that far, but you need some kind of variation in your tone. Some people will just try to go up and down at random, but the real way to vary your tone is to speak with passion and emotion. Listen to the popular motivational coach Tony Robbins; he is able to draw you in and hold your attention for hours at a time by speaking with passion and emotion *all the time.*

• Body movement

For larger groups, your feet shouldn't be rooted; you should be moving around. Shifting weight is bad when it's done because of nervousness, but in this case you want to keep moving around. Leaning, stepping and shifting weight are the main components here. The reason we gesture and move our bodies is because the eye is drawn to movement. If we are completely still whilst in-set, and we are in a venue with movement in the background, women's eyes will be drawn to that movement. When you lose eye contact with someone, they are paying less attention. Their eyes wander, they notice other things, and then their mind wanders.

• Facial animation

People will be drawn into what you say if you're more facially animated. Be expressive. Study others who do this well, and practise.

• Eye contact

To hold attention, spread your eye contact around the group; if you're losing one person, give them more attention. If you are holding eye contact with someone, and they are giving it back, they have to focus on you and what you are saying. If you don't look at them, they can look around the room, their attention will wander and you will lose connection. If you hold eye contact, even if they look around the room, they will feel drawn back to you because of it. If you find holding eye contact difficult, you can do what I did: I spent weeks making sure that, when I made eye contact in the street, coffee shop or on public transport, I wasn't the first to break it.

Energy levels can also be dynamically managed during an interaction. This is a more advanced use of energy levels, but what you're doing here is bringing up your energy levels when you notice that you're losing the attention of the group or individual members. You direct your gestures and eye contact towards the people in the set that are not paying as much attention, and bring them back in.

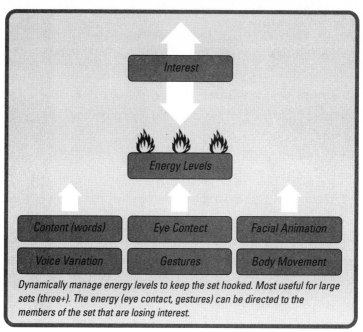

Dynamically manage energy levels to keep the set hooked. Most useful for large sets (three+). The energy (eye contact, gestures) can be directed to the members of the set that are losing interest.

The Three Characters
of a Seduction

I T DOESN'T GET MUCH SIMPLER THAN THIS. HERE ARE
THE STEPS YOU CAN USE TO IMMEDIATELY GET BETTER
RESULTS. I COULD STRING OUT THIS CHAPTER AND MAKE IT
INTO A BOOK — BUT JUST BECAUSE I HAVE MADE IT AS
SUCCINCT AS POSSIBLE, DON'T UNDERESTIMATE THE
IMPORTANCE. These are the three characters you can
assume during every interaction with women. No, it
doesn't mean acting, it just means being aware of how you
are presenting yourself at different stages of an
interaction. We all have different ways of behaving – with
our parents, our girlfriend, our friends. What we do here
is use our different ways of behaving to *consciously* progress
an interaction – or even an existing relationship – to the
next level.

MR. SOCIABLE, MR. COMFORT AND THE SEDUCER

Most guys have one character all the way through a seduction. For a fun-loving extrovert, it will be 'Mr. Sociable'. For most men, it will be 'Mr. Comfort', the nice guy who might be interesting once you get talking to him, but isn't particularly fun or sexual. The third is the sexual guy who goes in directly with a strong sexual vibe. These guys will get some results, but they won't be consistent. Once described in this way, it's pretty easy to see that you need a bit of each to be successful in any situation.

I was always Mr. Comfort. I found it hard to start the interactions, to make people laugh and to have fun with light banter. Once I was more comfortable in a conversation, I was good at making a strong connection with the girl – but unfortunately, I was also missing any kind of sexual vibe and had no idea how to escalate. I'd talk in this way for a while, and be thinking about going in for a kiss; the problem would be that the conversation had no sexual tension, so it would have been awkward and I'd have probably been rejected. Guys who also have this problem will be the oft-mentioned 'nice guy who finishes last', who the girls just want to be friends with. At work, I sometimes went with the team for lunch; they were all women, and they'd openly talk about sex and relationships in front of me. They did this because I was in no way sexual. They saw me as similar to the gay best friend, and could probably have got changed in front of me as if I were one of their girlfriends.

61

There is a point in an interaction where a woman makes the choice between seeing you as a friend or as a possible romantic interest. You need to be able to spice things up at this point to avoid going down the friend route. Over time and without any pre-planning, I developed my other two characters, Mr. Sociable and the Seducer, and my success rate with women increased hugely. To increase *your* success rate, you need to use the three characters as follows:

1. Mr. Sociable

This is the guy that makes a great first impression; he has high energy levels (see subsection on energy levels), is animated and makes people feel comfortable. He will be able to get in with any group, make them laugh and generally brighten up their evening. We are glad this person is around because there will be no awkward silences, he'll keep the conversation going.

Someone who is naturally Mr. Comfort might think too much about what he says; he thinks he's being considerate, but people relax a lot more when the person they are with is relaxed himself. Mr. Sociable personifies this because he is obviously being very natural, and saying what comes to mind. Because he is comfortable, people will relax around him. On the other hand, he will be very good for the first few minutes but might find it hard to connect with the person, or to seduce them, simply because he is too high-energy. After a while women will probably become tired of talking to him, because he can't be serious or deep. We've all been in situations with someone who constantly tries to crack jokes; it's good for a few minutes but quickly becomes tiresome. Use this character for the first few minutes until you're into a comfortable two-way conversation and they want you to stick around. Extroverts will find it easier to step into this character, whereas introverts will find it harder. I knew for a long time that I needed to be more sociable, outgoing, funny, and interesting – but how do you do that? Everyone can think of someone who is the archetypal Mr. Sociable, and to be him yourself you need to:

- Be high energy. Remember: voice-tone variation, body movement, eye contact, gestures, facial animation.

- Be positive. We like to moan about the weather, how stressed we are, how bad the food is, and whatever else. Although we can connect with people by talking about negative stuff, people would much prefer to be surrounded by those who make them feel good. Find the positive aspects, and if someone starts a negative conversational thread try to switch it as soon as possible. I'm not talking about being 'happy clappy'; you can be realistic but, if you have the choice of talking about something negative or positive, accentuate the positive.

- Enjoy yourself. Enjoy the music, the company, the venue, the drinks, the food. Most people don't seem to enjoy themselves much, but we are always drawn towards people that look like they are having fun.

Enthusiasm, passion and happiness are contagious. You will make people want to be part of your life if you look like you are enjoying yourself. One man might be a billionaire with the perfect life, but look bored and uninterested; another might be average in every regard, but have a real passion for life – women will want to be with him subconsciously, because this person can make them feel good.

- Smile. You'll already stand out, as most people don't smile!
- Do most of the talking. Ask few questions. Keep the conversation light and situational.

To develop this character, there are a few active steps and exercises you can undertake:

- Do something that involves public speaking and being the centre of attention – toastmasters club, TEFL course, stand-up comedy class, acting.
- Try this acting exercise with a friend: one-word impro. The way it works is that you try to make a story one word at a time: you say a word ('I') and then your friend says a word ('will') and you continue like this. (Go. And. See. My. Friends. At. The. Beach. And. Build. A. Sandcastle. Then . . .) When you come to a full-stop, you use words like 'next', 'afterwards' and 'then' to carry it on. You try to increase the speed and, when you get good at this, it should translate directly into natural conversation.

You can see this character at work in actors like Owen Wilson and Vince Vaughn in *Wedding Crashers*. I'd imagine that quick-witted TV hosts also could have the Mr. Sociable character down pat.

2. Mr. Comfort

After you've integrated into a group, you can bring out Mr. Comfort. When you first approach strangers, they are usually in a 'wait and see' mode. It might happen quickly, or might take a while, but soon they should open up to you and commit to the interaction. How do you know when this has happened? Non-verbally: they will stop looking at each other, or around the room, and will be focused on you and what you say. Verbally: they will start to commit more to the conversation, giving longer answers and asking you questions.

Mr. Comfort is interested and interesting. He listens fifty per cent of the time, doesn't talk too much about himself and tries to understand women, find common interests and build rapport. He should stick around until you've made a connection with a girl, at which point he should start to bring in some elements of the next character, the Seducer. Usually, Mr. Comfort cannot start conversations very well and is not very seductive, so it will be awkward when he goes in for the kiss. Being Mr. Comfort was always my strong point. Most introverts will be at home in this mode. The problem is getting stuck in it! Ninety per cent of the time, when guys tell me they have been put into the 'friend zone' by a woman, it's due to being Mr. Comfort for too long. Having no sexual vibe, no matter how good you are conversationally, means you're no more use than her girlfriends or gay best friend!

3. The Seducer

The Seducer, coming in after Mr. Sociable and Mr. Comfort, will be very effective. The following are behavioural traits of the Seducer:

- He looks at a woman in a way that tells her he wants her.
- He speaks more slowly, with a deeper voice.
- He touches her in increasingly sexual ways.
- He holds her hand when he talks.
- He holds intense eye contact.
- He is comfortable with pauses in the conversation.

The Seducer should smoothly emerge from Mr. Comfort as you find out more about the woman and become more attracted. When he is there from the start, it looks like you're just into her for her looks. By matching the way a woman becomes attracted to a man (generally, they warm up to a man over time), you'll separate yourself from other guys and she'll feel a deeper connection.

Learn the three characters of the seduction and you'll smoothly move from starting conversations to getting intimate. It's one of the most useful skills that you will learn.

MISSION THREE

You might be good at one or two of the characters, but need to work on the others. Sorry, but the best way is to use a mirror! You can also watch films, and see the transition in play. The woman is never going to feel turned on in the action scenes, just as she isn't with Mr. Sociable. She isn't going to feel turned on by the coffee-shop conversation, that's Mr. Comfort. Watching how actors escalate the mood by looking at her differently, and speaking in a seductive way, it's easy to see how this can apply in the real world! Become aware of yourself and practise your seductive looks in the mirror.

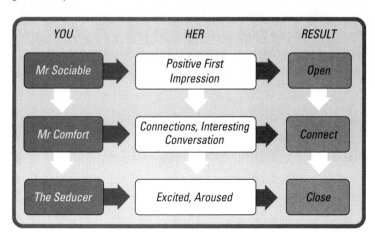

Making Things Easier

AFTER MONTHS OF GOING OUT, I REALISED THAT THERE WERE WAYS TO MAKE MY JOB OF ATTRACTING WOMEN MUCH EASIER. I COULD COLD-APPROACH A SEATED GROUP OF FIVE, ISOLATE ONE OF THEM, GO OFF SOMEWHERE AND GO FOR THE CLOSE. However, I learned that by only considering cold approaches I was missing out on a lot of much easier opportunities. I also realised that I could do certain things to increase my success rate on cold approaches, by increasing my value within a location first. The easiest approach is a warm approach; the second easiest is a cold approach in a location where you already have a lot of value. Here's how you make your approaches easier and maximise the chances of success:

OPENING COLD VS. OPENING WARM

A cold approach is when you open a girl and are unsure of the response you'll get. She has not shown interest in you and may not have even noticed you. A warm approach is one where you think the response will be at least somewhat positive because you've made eye contact or received some sign of interest. Obviously, if all our approaches could be warm approaches, the results would be a lot more successful. There are ways of increasing the ratio of warm to cold approaches and these are:

Standing out in a Positive Way

Being Mr. Sociable and talking to people *other than* the hottest women will disarm them. They'll see you having fun with people, and by the time you get near them they will be a lot more open and receptive. This is easier than trying to stand out in a club by being super-cool, since many other guys are trying to do the same.

Forcing Her Interest

Most guys deal with eye contact from a girl in one of three ways. What do you do? Do you nervously look away? Do you hold eye contact until she looks away? Do you force a smile? These are all pretty bad. You can still wonder why a girl was looking at you and use the uncertainty as an excuse not to approach. Maybe she was looking at someone else; maybe you have a spot on your nose; maybe she was just daydreaming. In ninety per cent of cases, she is looking at you and would welcome your approach, but there is always the other ten per cent and that is enough to discourage most guys from *ever* approaching! Here's what to do: force her interest! When you've got eye contact with the girl, provoke a response from her by doing something like pointing at her, waving, raising your glass, making a cheeky face or poking your tongue out. Personally, I do my trademark point; I guess it looks like something Joey from *Friends* would do. The girl is compelled to respond. The number of responses she can give is limited. She can:

- Mirror your action.
- Smile.
- Smile and look away, embarrassed.
- Look away in disgust.
- Turn up her lip as if to say, "What's he doing?"

If you get a positive reaction, you can approach straight away and don't need to think of anything clever to say. If you get a negative reaction, you probably won't get a good one when you open. Many of my girlfriends were initially approached after I had forced their interest. It's one of my best skills and makes my life a lot easier. It should become a reflex action, as if you had studied kung fu and you move without thinking when someone attacks you. It requires a lot less confidence to force a girl's interest than to approach cold.

APPROACHING AFTER AN INDICATION OF INTEREST

If she gave you a sign of interest, it's doubtful that she's not attracted, so go for it! I usually use "Hey, how's it going?" Longer or indirect openers (like asking for an opinion) will kill tension. Just be bold, direct and assume attraction.

MAXIMISING INTERACTIONS – TAKING EVERY OPPORTUNITY

In a club or bar environment, if you limit yourself to cold walk-ups, you're making things difficult for yourself. There are plenty of opportunities around you at all times to help create interactions:

Women stepping on your foot: "Hey, watch it, punk! [*squaring up with a smirk*] Let's take this outside, let me see what you've got!" Flex pose and point for her to do likewise – then feel the muscle.

Women squeezing past with drinks: "Cheers."

Women pushing past rudely: "No, my dear, do it like this: [*demo polite way to move past*] 'Excuse me, sir.'"

All these will allow you to get into interactions without the pressure and effort of a cold approach.

WORKING THE ROOM

Working the room in pick-up involves talking to all the groups you're interested in, as well as some other people in the room, all the time staying very indirect. At the end of a short interaction, the key is to make as if to leave and then, as if an afterthought, get the girl's name. What you'll be able to do in a short amount of time is:

- Meet and find the names of all the girls you are attracted to.
- Create a positive, safe, non-threatening impression in their heads – you are not so desperate that you have to stick in there until they tell you to go away.
- Establish yourself as Mr. Sociable.

After you've done this, you'll be able to re-open any of these groups at any time during the night. You'll also notice a big increase in interest from girls that you've already opened. Getting the name is the key factor. I found out by chance that re-opening with the name is much more effective, as the girl will actually treat you like someone she has known for a long time.

This technique is best used in smaller places, early on in the evening. That way, as the night progresses and people open up, your options will continue to increase. Plus you won't have the problem of opening when it gets noisier.

I used to work the room in a small Covent Garden club I went to regularly. Once, I arranged to meet a friend there, but picked up a girl on the way to the club and brought her with me. Now I was in the difficult position of being with a girl I wanted to spend time with, but also having to leave my poor friend on his own. I told her to wait for a minute, and I went with my friend around the whole club, said 'hi' to everyone, took their name, chatted for thirty seconds, introduced my friend and then went on to the next group. I did this to everyone in the club and, on the way back, literally every girl in the place was staring at me. I'd warmed up the whole club, and my friend could easily re-open any of the girls there. He used us as a base in the club, coming back between interactions, but was easily able to get a lot of numbers because he already had huge social proof as a fun-loving, sociable guy who seemed to know everyone. If he forgot a name, he could come back and ask me because I'd memorised all of them.

MISSION FOUR

Go to a bar, buy a drink (or get a tap water!) and go around 'cheers-ing' everyone. You will find that people will always 'cheers' you back, and that afterwards you get a lot of attention from girls wondering why you didn't try to pick them up. It's an easy way to work the room, and removes the need to think of anything to say!

EVOLUTION OF A NATURAL: JUNE 2006

One night in the Gardening Club, Covent Garden, I spotted a girl on the edge of the dance-floor. She was tall (six foot, in fact) and pretty, and we made eye contact. I said loudly to my friend as I pointed at her, "She's a cutie pie." She said,

"I'm a what?" I got in her face and said, "You're a cutie pie." I asked if she liked dancing; she said she did, and I said, "Do you salsa?" Before she had a chance to answer, I started to salsa with her. I asked her name, and made small talk as we danced, but there was a lot of sexual tension from the eye contact and dancing. After a few minutes, I touched her hair and slowly came in for a kiss. I took her off the dance-floor to the sofas and we had a really deep conversation about all kinds of things. After a while we were losing the sexual tension, so I put my finger to my lip, made the sign to "shhh" and kissed her some more. When the club closed, I said I wanted to show her where I lived and took her to my house. I didn't try anything on with her there. I guess I did it so that she would get comfortable at my place and return later. Then I walked her back home and we talked and kissed for an hour outside; then she invited me in. I stayed for a couple more hours and slowly escalated to sex. It took about three hours in her room to get there. She got horny, but I guess she was fighting with the belief that society had put in her head that she shouldn't sleep with a guy so quickly. It was quick, but it felt right!

Over the next couple of weeks, we had romantic picnics in the park, she stayed over at my house many times, and I stayed at hers. She introduced me to her friends and I did the same. On the surface, and in my mind, things were great. But, after three weeks, she became difficult to get hold of on the phone and sent me an email saying that she thought we should just be friends. She dumped me!

We were very different; she smoked cigarettes and weed and I didn't; she liked different food and different music, and had a different outlook on life. The funny thing was, instead of being solid in my own reality, I showed her that I would change for her. I downloaded the music *she* liked to my MP3 player, and even said I'd smoke weed with her. I called her every day, and this became a problem. She had her friend come and visit, and the friend got pissed off with her because she was spending time with me. I was always available. She dumped me after three weeks because I liked her more than she liked me; I looked at her like I loved her, and she felt stifled.

The funniest thing was that, a few months after she dumped me, I found a recording on my MP3 player; it was the last conversation we had on the last day that I saw her, it must have accidentally switched on in my pocket. I could barely listen to it – not because it brought back sad memories, but because of how weak, needy and unattractive I sounded. I was seeking approval, validation, letting her take charge, asking her to "please stay longer", asking when we could meet again. It was sickening. I was breaking all the rules I'd learned and knew very well. I was doing what so many men do. Women become so important to us, and this is how we act when we finally get one. The knowledge wasn't enough to stop me making the mistakes.

After she dumped me, I was crushed for two weeks. I thought that every time I was in love with a girl she'd dump me.

DIRECT OR INDIRECT? BOTH!

There are two very distinct schools of seduction, direct or indirect, and most methods will fall into one of them. This system takes both into account and I suggest that you use them both.

Direct Game

Direct game involves approaching, immediately conveying interest, then rapidly intensifying the interaction with words and kino-escalation. An example of direct game is to approach a girl, tell her you think she is beautiful, then take her by the hands and increase physical contact. You're basically approaching in seduction mode (see 'The Three Characters of a Seduction'). The benefit of a direct approach is its efficiency. It allows you to quickly test a girl's interest. Who wants to wait hours to kiss if they don't have to? Who wants to chat for an hour before finding out the girl is unavailable?

The drawbacks of direct game are that:

- It requires a high degree of personal and sexual confidence in order to be successful.
- It generates more approach anxiety by putting you on the line and adding pressure to the interaction.
- You may be rejected from a group that would have been receptive to a more subtly slow approach.
- Women generally need more time to warm up to a guy, and consider the initial first impression as less important than a man does.

76

Indirect Game

Indirect game is basically coming in under the radar, getting the girl comfortable with you and slowly introducing the sexual vibe. The benefits of an indirect approach are:

- Less approach anxiety by minimising the chance of getting blown out.
- Easier with an all-girl or mixed group.
- More and longer interactions, which allow you to get comfortable talking to women and to practise your conversation skills.

The drawbacks of an indirect approach are:

- Sometimes she wants you and you lose her because she doesn't think you're interested.
- You can waste time on a girl who you have no chance with (she'll never find you attractive, she is engaged, she is a lesbian), and you don't find out because she thinks you're just being friendly.

Use direct game when you're getting a clear sign of interest. If you're not quite sure, take the indirect route. You should also ensure that your approaches remain indirect until you have a lot of experience reading situations and have overcome any approach anxiety. If I have a client who has a huge fear of talking to women, I'll ensure his first few approaches involve doing things like asking for directions – this is as indirect as you can get.

The System –
From Open to Close

THE IMPORTANT THING I WANT TO COMMUNICATE IS NOT THAT MY METHOD OF SEDUCTION IS BETTER THAN ANY OTHER, OR THAT THIS IS *THE* METHOD FOR ATTRACTING WOMEN. It is that I think it's necessary to have the structure of a seduction in your head any time you're in an interaction with a woman you like. This allows you to be aware of what you're doing and what you need to do next. I have designed my system to be simple enough to learn and understand in under an hour, and from then on it can be remembered at a moment's notice.

'The System' refers to a somewhat indirect approach in a day- or night-time environment. It involves an opener and a transition from the opener. You should have these two prepared when you are starting out. Next, use 'Skills of the Natural' until you reach a point where she has opened up enough to give more to the conversation. This could be immediately, but you may need to do most of the talking until they are comfortable enough to have a conversation with you. At this point you can ask more questions and go into the rapport stage.

There is a goal at every step. Initially, the goal is to get them committed to the interaction. You know when you've hooked them because girls will do one or more of the following:

• Open up their body language to you.
• Stop looking at each other and focus on you.
• Ask you questions or make other attempts to extend the interaction.
• Give fuller responses to what you say.

Once the 'hook point' has been reached we switch to the next goal, which is to use rapport to find common interests and use the universal transitions to find out their current situation. Achieving this will put us in a better position in order to number close.

Next comes the rapport stage, which puts you in a better position to get a close. During deep rapport, you need to get a strong connection with the girl and make her see you're someone who understands her. Kino-escalation is necessary to have some sexual tension so that you avoid being a 'friend'. It allows you to test the water by gradually increasing the intimacy of the touch leading up to the kiss.

Understanding the System and following it from open to

close will greatly increase your success rate, because you'll be constantly focused on the goals you will need to achieve step by step.

THE THREE CHARACTERS OF A SEDUCTION AND THE SYSTEM

How do you apply the three characters within the System? Mr. Sociable should be used until you reach the hook point. Mr. Comfort should start to come in at this point, especially if you and she are alone. The Seducer can come in after some connections have been made in preparation for a physical close. Don't think of the transitions as 'on' and 'off', but as sliders that allow you to smoothly flow from one to another.

EVOLUTION OF A NATURAL: JULY 2006

I had a one-on-one day with my fourth client one night, and for the first time I met a girl I was interested in on a training session. We were in Cheers bar in Piccadilly on a Thursday night and, after showing him some methods, I sent him to approach a girl. Now, my job in this situation was to watch him so that I give could him feedback, and to deal with any of her friends that were there, so that he could interact with her one on one. Amazingly, her friend turned out to be a very hot French girl. It really makes a difference to a guy's mind when he sees a beautiful girl; I was nervous and excited, but had learned not to show my nerves on the outside.

I started by sitting opposite her. I quickly told her it was too loud to talk across the table and that we should sit next to each other. We had a fantastic conversation, during which I found out she played the harp and painted. I connected with her on both these points, just as I describe in the chapters on rapport and connecting. I took her number and arranged to see her in a couple of days. It was pretty simple, with minimal touching, but a good conversation.

I called her in the daytime, arranged to meet at night, and met her at the tube station near my house. When I came to meet her, she was already being chatted up by a couple of guys. (I overheard one say that he liked her bag!) I took her to a pub and sat next to her; because she was very beautiful, I had trouble escalating physically and being playful. Another tendency I had with very attractive girls was to give them so much status that I would play it safe and not take risks (like touching or taking the piss) for fear of being rejected. We chatted and got on very well. She was only nineteen years old and had come to London with no job; now she was sharing a room with her friend and working as a waitress. She had some very attractive qualities and some interesting life history. She told me that she had a sailboat in France, and would sail out into the lake and fall asleep looking at the stars. We made a great connection. When I find someone very attractive and I'm interested in them, I connect naturally and deeply. I had the night all planned out, because I'd got some advice from Steve. I wanted to sleep with her as soon as possible, because as I'd learned that if you like the girl it makes the relationship easier, so you should get the first time out of the way as quickly as possible; if you only like her physically, you also want to do it quickly! The pub closed at 11.00 and I led her back to my house. When we got to the door she asked where we were, and I told her I was going to show her where I lived.

We were sitting in my room on the bed (because there's no lounge and the bed is the only place to sit) and there was a beautiful moment when she revealed something very personal. She told me that her harp was a 'he' and, when the window was open, 'he' would make sounds from the wind that she thought was him talking to her, and she would play a response. She told me she had never told someone about it before, but that she felt I understood her and it was like she had known me for three months.

I put my glass of wine down, moved towards her, ran my fingers through her hair and went in to kiss her. She turned her head to the side! Instead of backing off, I kissed her cheek and then her neck and then turned her head back. At this point she went crazy and jumped on top of me and started kissing me aggressively and biting my lips. This had never happened before. I couldn't really handle it and didn't like it. There was a moment when I saw her face looking like it wanted to devour me, and I was scared! I had only had slow, soft and tender moments, and this girl wanted to be fucked. She wanted a confident, dominant man, and I had seemed to be that guy when I picked her up, but I didn't yet have the sexual confidence. I got on top of her and pinned her down, but it was tentative and I didn't really know what I was doing. She wanted me to control her physically and loved it when I did. I'd never ripped a girl's clothes off and had wild sex before. I was a bit slow for her liking and, though we did get it on, I was in my head all the time, thinking about what I should do to make her happy and not really enjoying the moment as I should have been.

I felt like it was my problem, and that a real man would have been able to handle the situation properly. I'd known that I wasn't very manly for a while. When I was at work from eighteen to twenty years old, I was the 'friend' who posed no sexual threat, someone that didn't project any sexuality. I'd sit around with the marketing department girls, and they'd talk about sex and personal issues as if *I* were a girl. When I was with my friends, I didn't talk about sex or women in the usual crass way. I don't think it is necessary to do that – but it *is* necessary to be sexually confident and to be able to handle sexually aggressive women without being scared off. Women should see you as sexual, not as a gay best friend!

I'd been brought up by my mother with no male influences or role models, and I guess I lacked a general manliness and (especially) sexual confidence. I had learned the attributes of an alpha male and definitely projected them in a club, but I did have a weak underbelly and it revealed itself in the bedroom! The French girl was only nineteen but I couldn't handle her. She said, "Yes, I like sex," and was very matter-of-fact about it. I was happy to have slept with her, she was one of the best-looking girls I'd met in London, but I know I didn't really give her what she wanted!

After this night, I started to chase her; I knew that she was sexual and would be having sex with someone, and I wanted it to be me. I called her and we met one more time before she started work. I was quite needy; I think she sensed that I wanted a relationship when she really didn't, so after that she didn't return my calls and we didn't sleep together again. Again, I was upset about it, but not as much as when the Serbian girl dumped me. Because this time I thought about what I did wrong, decided what I should have done and wrote it down. When I looked at it, I realised that the same thing wasn't going to happen again and I felt instantly better.

THE FIRST MINUTE

The first minute of a pick-up is the most important. In this time, you will have identified a target, got into state, overcome any approach anxiety, positioned yourself, opened and hopefully achieved a hook point. Normally, by the end of the first minute you know how receptive the target is, and whether or not you have a realistic chance of success.

THE POWER OF 'HEY' AS A PRE-OPENER

Why do all openers start with 'Hey'? This is an important point that needs to be explained. If you deliver an opener to a woman or a group, most of the time you're interrupting them. They will likely be in conversation already, or at least thinking about something with a conversation going on inside their head. When you start talking, you're breaking that state and their response will be, "What?" They will say, "What?" even if they have heard what you've said. Think about how you do this in your own life. I only learned this properly when I started as a trainer and watched students open without saying "Hey" – the girls would say, "What?" and the interaction always seemed to go badly after that. It got them off on the wrong foot from the beginning. The 'Hey' is followed by a pause, to ensure that you have the attention of the group *before* you deliver your opener. It's "Hey!" (*Pause. Group looks at you.*) "Do you guys . . ." The pre-opener can be anything that gets the attention of the group: "Hey!" "Oi!" "Yo!" "Howdy!" or even something non-verbal, like a finger click, an expression or some other action that makes them stop what they are doing and look at you.

OPENING AND TRANSITIONING

Friends are always asking me what the best openers are, but what they don't realise is that the transition is actually more important than the opener. The most important thing is what you follow the opener with. That's why, until you can freestyle using 'Skills of the Natural', you need to know your opener and also the transition before you start an interaction. If you open with, "Hey, should I dye my hair blond?" and they say, "Yes," and you say, "OK, thanks, bye," that's not too good. You need to know what you'll follow it up with. So you can use that opener and then your transition is: "Cool, because my hairdresser tells me every time I go there that I'd look great with blond hair, he's a great hairdresser. But he's gay, so I really wasn't sure on this one. Actually, I say he's gay because I just think he is, but he tries to talk about women. He just looks gay. Do you think you can tell when a man is gay?" If you go in with that much prepared, you have enough to get to the hook point in the majority of cases. If you just have the opener ready, you'll be putting a lot more pressure on yourself.

Personally I don't think the opener is that important, and I prove this with students by asking for the lamest opener possible and still showing that I can hook or close. An example would be: "My elbow hurts," which was one given to me by a one-on-one student who just didn't believe that the opener wasn't important. I went into a seated pair of girls without knowing what I'd come up with as a transition, and actually used: "I was testing the theory that you can use anything to start a conversation." They were initially very negative, but even after this opener they opened up after a minute or so; I stayed for fifteen minutes and number-closed one of them. I could also have used: "I'm taking acting classes and wanted to see if I could make you believe my elbow actually hurt." The transition also needs to be as solid as possible. If it's weak it shouldn't be dwelt on – change subjects quickly.

EVOLUTION OF A NATURAL: JULY–AUGUST 2006

One day in July, my new friend Steve, who I had known for a few weeks, asked if he could come to my house to use the internet because his laptop was broken. He came to book his ticket to Sweden, and was planning a subsequent tour of the whole of Eastern Europe before flying to Asia, and finally to South America. He'd decided to take six months to a year off from work. While he was on Ryanair's website, he looked over and asked me if I'd like to come. I asked him when, he said in two weeks and I said, "Sure." I'd never spent more than a few hours with this guy, but I'd committed to going on holiday for two months with him. I'd also just started a business, and had obligations like my rent to take care of. However, I love to travel, and I'd also decided that the new me would be spontaneous. I'd finally moved to London, and I was starting to achieve more on the basis of taking action every time there was an opportunity.

I put everything on hold and we flew to Stockholm in late July. A big part of this trip was going to be checking out the local girls in these countries. Yes, we did see the sights, enjoy the food and learn some of the languages, but we also went out on forty nights out of forty-four (the four that we didn't were when we were travelling overnight by boat, train or coach). We went to Sweden, Finland, Estonia, Latvia, Lithuania, Belarus, Ukraine, Moldova, Romania, Hungary, and flew back from Slovakia. It was a long trip, but these are the highlights:

- Latvia has the most beautiful women in the world. Honourable mentions go to Lithuania and Sweden.

- It helps if you can speak just a few words. I studied Pimsleur Swedish on the flight over and Pimsleur Russian on the coach to Latvia, and was able to impress people – not with my language skills, but in that I'd made an effort. (Especially true in Sweden, where they all speak English anyway.)

- Russians and men from the former USSR are tough, they will kick your ass! They don't dance, you will think the girls are on their own, and suddenly a big dude will come over to you. I saw it happen in Lithuania where an American guy nearly got beaten up, giving me a severe case of approach anxiety that night.

- The countries are safe and the nightclubs are much better designed than in London!

- Some countries like foreigners, some don't. Latvia, Estonia and Lithuania have been spoiled by lager-lout stag parties coming over on cheap flights looking for girls. The result is that the reputation of the English gentleman is gone, and it is considered a bad thing to be seen getting physical, or even talking to, a foreigner in those countries. The girl might fancy you, but social pressure will stop her acting on it. I thought I might be able to play the Italian card (being half-Italian), but Italians were even less popular. I spoke to some Italian guys and they helped me understand why. When I asked why they were in Riga, the Latvian capital, they said, "Italian guys are here to fuck!" Great. Anyway, the only fucking for them was in the brothels, because I never saw another foreigner pull in a Riga club!

My game improved a lot during the trip. I was with Steve, who was a natural, and we had no pressure or responsibility so we were just out having fun. We were surrounded by a lot of beautiful girls. One day I walked around Riga, and needed to take a lie-down and avert my eyes because of the sensory overload. It was like being on another planet. When we went to clubs like the ones in Riga, where the standard of beauty was so outrageously high, it put us in a fantastic mood – which is exactly the right state to be in.

I didn't speak the local languages and we were mostly going to nightclubs. This meant that two areas of my game improved massively – non-verbal escalation and dance-floor game. Prior to the trip, I really wasn't comfortable on the dance-floor. I had done my four salsa lessons, but I was still very uncoordinated and, more than anything else, very self-conscious. Why do we all think everybody is looking at us when we are on the dance-floor? Why are we even thinking about this, living in our head rather than feeling the vibe and following the beat? Who knows, but the answer is to:

- Go out with someone who doesn't give a shit and just dances, even if they have no moves.
- Do it a bunch of times – it aids desensitisation.

Non-verbal game enabled me to kiss a girl with no words; then, a few minutes later, she'd say something to me in Russian and find out I didn't even speak her language. When it is noisy and people don't all speak English, you are forced to communicate using gestures and facial expressions. (Not miming exactly, just subtle looks and actions which show that you like her.) You do this, she smiles, you dance together, you kiss. Simple, and all without words – although there is no easy way to develop this skill unless you lose your voice for a few weeks, or just throw yourself into it like I did.

The other thing that happened was that I got desensitised to very beautiful women, and so could be more cool and relaxed when dealing with them. When I was back in London, I could no longer be intimidated by a beautiful woman.

Opening

THE OPENER IS THE FIRST THING YOU SAY DURING AN INTERACTION. THE BEST OPENERS MAKE HER LAUGH, MAKE YOU LOOK COOL, AND ARE MUCH MORE INTERESTING THAN WHATEVER THE GIRLS WERE DISCUSSING BEFORE YOU CAME ALONG. There are various types of openers. An indirect opener is one that doesn't immediately convey your interest in her, and doesn't put much pressure into the interaction. If you say, "You're hot and I want you," that would be very direct and would put a lot of pressure on her; if you say, "When does it get busy here?" there is no pressure. Opinion openers work very well in bars and quiet clubs; time and time again I've seen them successfully hook a group.

INDIRECT

Here are some indirect openers and how they might be used. Different people feel comfortable saying different things. You can pick a few from below, modify one and later make up your own. You don't need hundreds. A couple of solid tried and tested openers are enough.

Oh, there is a guy over there who is so perfect for you!
This opener involves approaching a woman, pointing to a guy you think is 'perfect' for her, and trying to take her over to meet him. Invariably she'll refuse, and then you can say how she should trust you because you're a great matchmaker. It leads nicely into conversation on dating and relationships. Her objection is projected on to the other guy, so you've less chance of getting rejected. It also provides a false disqualifier for you, ultimately making it easier to hook a group.

You are so . . . in my way.
If you're in a situation where you're walking and a girl blocks your path, put your hand up as if to gesture for her to stop. Look at her seriously and deliver the line. The key is the pause; it makes her think you're going to say, "You are so beautiful" or some other clichéd statement. If you do it right, it guarantees a laugh. I used to use it when I first started, and they'd laugh but still carry on walking afterwards – so you should quickly introduce yourself to extend the opening.

THE NATURAL ART OF SEDUCTION

Are you guys sociable/friendly?
Standard opener, can be delivered with a sceptical face. Be ready for a yes or no answer and have a follow-up ready.

Are you guys super-shy or what? I've been here for ten minutes and you haven't offered to buy me a drink or even said hello.
This one puts them on the spot slightly and then releases the tension; they will laugh if it's delivered right.

Are you posh girls? Are you rich?
This allows the funny follow-up, "I'm looking for a rich, posh girl who can buy me stuff." I used this successfully, but, as with all the other one-liners, don't expect it to be a magic bullet. You still need to work a bit more to reach the hook point.

Did you invite all these people? I thought it'd just be us.
This is a semi-direct approach.

I know you probably get no attention from guys whatsoever, so I thought I'd come and make some conversation with you.
This one should get a laugh. You'll be on the spot after this, so have something to follow it up with.

[clothing primp] *What's your name?*
This one is good for a girl with a hat or some other kind of accessory. You look at her, double-take, look at the item and screw your face up as if something is wrong. Hold out

a finger to say "wait", adjust the item then study her again and make a thumbs-up. Don't let the opener end there, otherwise that'll be it. Follow it up with something like:

> You: What's your name?
> Her: Tanya.
> You: Tanya, I've just made you thirty-eight per cent more attractive, you owe me!

Hey, I'm out meeting people tonight, what's your name?
Standard, pretty low-risk opener that fits a Mr. Sociable frame.

Is this area of floor taken?
This is a funny play on "Is this chair taken?" Other variations include (park) "Is this area of grass taken?"

"Get ready!" "Huh?" "We are going to chat you up."
What you do here is tell the girls that you're going to chat them up. You can add something like, "I don't know how many times you've been chatted up but this is going to be the best ever, you should really be sitting down!" You then do a little bit of whispering and come in with the lamest chat-up line ever – something like, "Is God missing an angel because you're here?" Deliver it with a horridly unconfident delivery. Letting them reject that version of you gets past their bitch-shield and offsets their objections. You can then start talking about meeting girls in bars, picking up and dating in general. Ask questions about what the best and worst approach ever was.

Are you undressing me with your eyes?
If a girl is making eye contact with you, this is a good opener to use. Accusing them of stalking you, checking you out, etc. is a very good technique.

My girlfriend thinks you're hot.
Uses fake social proof to make it easier to open. Point to some random hot girl as your 'girlfriend'. Later it can be revealed that she is just a female friend, and you're in fact single – although you're friends with lots of girls.

Are you guys making mischief over here?
This is a funny one, and the delivery is important: suspicion mixed with playfulness works well. Say they look shifty, like they are going to steal something. This is another one I used successfully on a number of occasions.

My friend wants to know if you think I'm hot.
A fairly direct opener that offsets the direct question by asking it from a friend's point of view.

I know that look, are you guys male-bashing?
When you see women talking seriously, you can open with this. Chances are they are talking about men, and so will laugh. If not, they'll still probably laugh because they know that they often *are* male-bashing.

I saw you checking me out. I knew that, if I didn't confront you, you'd be following me around all night and trying to follow me home . . . I don't need another stalker.

How's it going? We're out picking up chicks.

Why didn't you call me?

[suspicious] *You look familiar, did we have sex?*
This one is very funny, but more for the guy delivering it than the girl. I like it a lot, but there are much more effective lines.

Are you listening to our conversation? Then why are you acting so nervous?
This is a good way to open a group who are standing near you. You can follow up with: "So what do you think?"
    "About what?"
    "About what we were talking about."
    "We weren't listening!"
    "Okay, well, we were talking about whether . . ." Into an opinion opener.

Which of you guys gets hit on the most?
This is a pretty good opener on two attractive girls that look kind of different from each other.

Are you confident enough to accept a sincere compliment? Good, so am I, you go first.
This is a classic, it will usually make them laugh. However, it can sometimes fall flat after they do, so make sure you have something ready to follow up with.

Are you single? So when are you asking me out? Are you nervous?
This one works very well because it puts the girl on the spot and gets her frustrated. You can then release it by nudging her and laughing or saying, "Wow, you're really cute when you're angry." You want to fire the questions in quick succession without giving her much time to think or answer fully.

If I didn't have a girlfriend and wasn't gay, you'd so be mine.
This is a variation on saying you're either gay or have a girlfriend. I think this one is better, because most people do not want to mislead a girl into thinking they are gay *or* have a girlfriend. It's also confusing, but her subconscious will get it that you're actually saying, "Be mine."

[big table] *"Hey, sorry I'm late."*
How the hell do you approach a big group who are waiting in the street, or sitting at a table in a bar/club? In this way: Talk about how the traffic was terrible; you're Paul's cousin/Bob's nephew/whatever. It's funny. When you get caught out, don't dwell on it, ask some names and find out what's going on, then proceed as normal.

97

Which of you girls is the toughest?

You have very thoughtful eyes. I think you have a lot going on inside here [touch head].
This is a good direct line to use on a girl who looks bored. Most guys go in with, "You look bored." That's never going to work, but this is a nice direct compliment.

Hey, I have a policy of meeting the hottest girl in the club when I go out. My name's Rich [shake hands].
Nice opener that has proved successful for me consistently.

Hey, I have a policy of meeting the hottest girl in the club when I go out. My name's Rich [shake hands]. *So, do you know her?* [point at another hot girl]
Cheekier, funnier, doesn't work as well for me! Girls don't usually get it.

OPINION OPENERS

Opinion openers are the easiest way for a newbie to open in a quiet bar/club. They are good in that they can get a long conversation started pretty easily. A well-crafted opinion opener can guarantee you a few minutes of conversation. The way to deliver it is to either make it seem spontaneous or to 'root' it. A spontaneous one comes from reacting to something your friend supposedly said and asking whoever is nearest, who just happen to be a pair of hot chicks! Rooting the opener means that you need to tell them the reason you're asking, so that they know why they are spending their time giving you their advice.

Jealous Girlfriend Routine

You: Hey, guys, let me get your opinion on something. I'm trying to give my friend over there advice, but we're just a bunch of guys and not qualified to comment on these matters. Okay, well, my friend has been dating a girl for three months. And she just moved in with him. Now, this is a two-part question. So, imagine you've been dating someone for three months. And he is still friends with his old girlfriend from college. How do you feel about that?

Hot Chicks: Answer.

You: Yes, they're *just* friends. There's nothing else going on. They talk like once a week at most.

HCs: I think it's fine/I don't think they should be talking/whatever.

You: Okay, now let's say that he has a drawer in his apartment. And in that drawer he keeps all of his old photographs and letters. Now, some of those letters happen to be from exes and some of the photographs happen to be with exes.

HCs: blah blah blah – concerned comment – blah blah blah – question

You: It's not like he ever looks at them. They are just there, like old souvenirs and memories of his past.

HCs: I think it's fine/I think he should put them away in a closet/ destroy them/whatever.

You: Okay, the reason I'm asking is because my friend's girlfriend says she doesn't want him to talk to his ex from college at all. She wants him to cut it off completely. And she wants him to destroy all of his old photos and letters from exes. She says it's just holding on to the past and he should let go of it now. Personally, I thought it was extreme and a bit insecure. But what do I know. I'm a guy. And, as we all know, guys think differently from girls . . .

Piercings

I deliver this one as follows: "Guys, what do you think of piercings? Because my ex-girlfriend was a bit of a rock chick and she always used to say [*pinching eyebrow to show where it would go*], 'You should get a piercing.' I'm not going out with her any more, but I'm still kinda considering it. Do you think piercings are sexy?" This one goes into different areas of male attractiveness and exactly what they consider attractive in a man.

Do I look gay?

This one is a killer. It never seems to fail. The root is that a guy just tried to pick you up, or your friend said you look gay in those shoes/that shirt. An alternative follow-up is to say that you were at the bar (doesn't even have to be that night) and that you got chatted up. They will laugh, and it just works a charm. The first time I tried this was on a

Scottish girl and her mum(!); it was a great approach and they opened up very easily. Since then I've used it very successfully, as have loads of my students.

Do you think Derren Brown/David Blaine is sexy?

The follow-up is to say that you've been studying magic/psychic stuff/ESP or whatever, and that you wondered whether it was their looks or their abilities that made them sexy to some women. It leads into any skill you profess to have, or any routine you can perform, in these areas.

Do you believe in palm reading/handwriting analysis?

Follow with "Me, too," or "I didn't either, but then . . ." and go into a story about a relative who does it for a living and showed you some stuff. "I was sceptical, but I brought my friend along and they got everything right. I'm not entirely sold, but I've been learning it a bit and want to see if it's a way to get to know people better, more quickly." This is a nice way to open and lead into one of these areas in a smooth way.

How soon is too soon to get engaged?

"You look like you can help me with this. My friend is coming in an hour and he needs my advice. He has known his girlfriend for three months and he is going to ask her to marry him, tomorrow. He says he wants my advice, but I think he has already made his mind up. I think it's too soon, but if I tell him that he might disown me. But if I say it's a good idea and it doesn't work out, I'll feel responsible. So what do you guys think, how soon is too soon to get engaged?" This is a fantastic opener that leads straight into relationship talk and has a lot of drama built in. It should hook very well.

My friend's girlfriend deleted all the pics of them kissing from his digital camera, you think that means anything?

I'd further classify opinion openers into 'spontaneous seeming' and 'walk-up strength'. If you have three girls sitting in the corner and need to go to them to make an approach, it'd seem strange to go out of your way only to ask if they think you look gay. However, using "How soon is too soon…?" will work very well. Generally, you need a more serious opener for a walk-up.

DIRECT OPENERS

It took a while before I had the confidence to deliver a direct opener. You need internal confidence; you have to believe in what you say and put yourself on the line. You have to have complete authority. If there is a hint of weakness and she picks up on it, the opener will fall flat. When you have confidence from your success with other openers, or if you're confident because you can tell the girl is attracted to you, bring out the direct opener and it'll be fantastic. You will receive super-fast results and women will think you're incredible because of your boldness. With a direct opener, if she doesn't respond negatively take the direct route and escalate quickly. Here are some examples:

I know this is kind of random, but I had to tell you that you're just too cute.

Do you know who you remind me of? Someone I want to meet.

I saw you and I knew that, if I didn't come and introduce myself, I'd never get to meet you, my name's...

I like you/You're beautiful. And I'm going to get to know you.

For more openers, check out the PUATraining Blog.

SITUATIONAL

These are what I mainly use now at the time of writing. A situational opener is taking something about the current situation and using that to start the interaction. It could be noticing something about her, but usually it's noticing something about the environment and saying the first question that comes to mind: "How can they eat ice cream in the winter?" "Would you wear *that?*" "Which one do you think is healthier?" I know when I have used a situational opener, because, when I try to remember which opener I did use, I can't. It's so natural and unconscious and uncalculated that it slips my mind. The way to be as natural and comfortable as possible is to get used to just saying whatever comes into your head, without delay or planning.

MISSION FIVE

Write down three openers you like, then go out and open ten sets. Your goal is just to open and stay as long as you are comfortable, make an excuse to leave, get their name and eject. This is to help you get comfortable with opening sets. You will notice that, as you become more comfortable, the interactions naturally last longer.

EVOLUTION OF A NATURAL: SEPTEMBER 2006

While I was away on holiday I had plenty of business ideas. I came back with lots of energy and enthusiasm and was ready to rock and roll. I'd lost my phone in Belarus, so there was no way to contact any of the girls whose numbers I'd taken before I left. But I had come back with renewed enthusiasm, big plans and greatly increased skills with the ladies. I also started to get some interesting opportunities. In September I received an email from someone who would become very important. It went something like this:

"Tell me to f*ck off if you like, but your website looks shit. I'm the daddy of web design, but I'm terrible with women. Maybe we can come to some kind of arrangement."

We talked on the phone and I arranged to meet him. Vince was a tall, good-looking guy, but he said he was abysmal with women. We worked out a deal: he would fix up my website, and I would get him laid! We arranged to meet for his first training session one night; I broke down some theory at my house and then took him to a club.

On the way, he spotted a girl he found attractive and I started to approach her, but he grabbed me and said, "*Nooo*." It was strange, he was so scared that he didn't even want *me* to approach a girl. We went to the club and he said he felt uncomfortable without his jacket on, that he thought his feet were too big, that he didn't know what to do with his arms because they were too long (a common problem for tall people). He couldn't hold eye contact, and if people were laughing he thought they were laughing at him.

I told him we wouldn't talk to any women that night and would just chill out. I chatted with him and just wanted him to get comfortable being in a club. My first mission for him was to start holding eye contact both with me and with girls. He would look at the girl until she looked away, instead of him breaking eye contact first. I also gave him some homework, to work on his psychology.

Next time we met, he was happy because he had held eye contact with girls and they had looked away first; he felt more powerful and confident. Next we took him to the same club again; I'd brought my cousin Alistair along as well, to help out. We built him up, told him all the positive things about himself, gave him more theory, and this time, in the club, kept him close by as we chatted to girls. It's like when someone is scared of dogs and you slowly desensitise them, getting them closer and closer to bigger and bigger dogs!

He'd be at the table and we'd be talking to the girls; if he wanted he could jump in and say something. That night I also did something else for him. I approached the rudest, drunkest-looking girl and did a sleazy "come here baby" kind of face; she told me to go away; I stuck around and did it again; she got louder and louder and was screaming, "Fuck off, you bastard!" I stood there for a minute, completely unresponsive, and then went back to him. I told him that that was the worst that could happen, and that I was still alive and would never see that girl again. The best that could happen was that you brought lovely women into your life and became happy.

We gave Vince a free pass to our bootcamps and he enjoyed hanging out with the boys, meeting the students and coming out with us at night. After a few weeks, he could confidently start conversations with girls, and had lost ninety per cent of his concerns – he no longer had problems with his appearance, he didn't think people were laughing at him, and he didn't worry about what they thought. Most importantly, he was comfortable and confident in most situations.

We had spent the first month ironing out his psychological issues, but we hadn't really worked on his skill with women. Over the next few weeks, we got him through the process that I had gone through and all the sticking points, but in an accelerated timeframe. He became comfortable starting conversations, carrying them on for longer and longer until he reached the point where he could get numbers. But he still hadn't kissed a girl in a club, or escalated physically. One night in Tiger Tiger, things seemed different; Vince was confident now, walking around the place and getting more attention than I was! His natural good looks were now matched by an internal confidence which made women really notice him. This is something I see time and time again – you can add points to your attractiveness simply by what you think of yourself. I opened a hot Argentinean girl, but I could tell that she was attracted to Vince, so I gave her my coat to hold (to keep her there) and stepped back. He did well, starting to touch her toned belly and playfully escalate things with her, but after ten minutes he lost it and the interaction ended. He told me he didn't know how to get the kiss. I gave him some tips right there and then. A few days later, we were at Onanon and Vince had had an interaction at the bar with a cute English girl. She met his criteria of being tall and slim and he was very interested in her. He came to me and asked what he should do; I told him that she wanted him and to try the hugging or dancing kiss close. This is what happened:

He grabs her as she goes past, brings him close to her, makes some small talk and then says, "Do you prefer hugging or dancing?" She says hugging and he hugs her. He waits a minute and then asks, "Do you prefer hugging or kissing?" She smiles and doesn't say anything, so he kisses her!

It might sound stupid, but in that moment I felt more happy than I had for months – and I'd had lots of personal success in that time. I'd seen Vince as someone who was unhappy with his life. I thought I could help him, but you can never be one hundred per cent sure. I'm happy when my clients do well, but I don't know all their history and I don't spend that much time with them. I considered Vince a good friend by this time, and it was a fantastic moment when I saw he had got what we wanted and would have this ability for the rest of his life.

Mid-Game

S O YOU'VE OPENED AND STARTED THE CONVERSATION. NEXT YOU NEED TO PROGRESS THINGS TO THE POINT WHERE YOU CAN NUMBER-CLOSE. A key element here will be 'Skills of the Natural', improving your small talk to the point where you give the woman a unique conversational experience.

SKILLS OF THE NATURAL – OPENER TO HOOK POINT TO RAPPORT

After the opener, we can purely use skills of the natural to get to the point of a number close. A number close requires a certain amount of rapport and connection. For anyone who wants to become a natural with women, and feels like they've always had that innate ability, this is the section to pay attention to.

I used to be a terrible conversationalist. I was boring on dates, useless in groups, a terrible public speaker and unable to hold people's attention. Now I game like a natural. This means that I'm able to break down exactly what's necessary to be a naturally good conversationalist and to generate attraction. I can give you exercises to practise this skill.

During the first minute of an interaction, you need to do most of the talking. Anything that puts the conversational pressure on her is something that she could use as an excuse to end the interaction. When she is comfortable and committed to the interaction (which could be instantly, but generally takes longer from a cold approach), you can start putting some of the conversational burden on her.

The art of small talk

Women are sick of boring conversations with men. They have had the same ones over and over and over. If you can be different, you'll stand out hugely and quickly generate attraction. But first, what *shouldn't* you do if you're a good conversationalist?

Hairdresser conversation

What kind of conversation do you have with a hairdresser, a person in line at the post office, or your aunt who you see once every six months? It's probably boring and shallow, what I like to call 'conversation on rails'. We have the conversation but we aren't really listening, we don't really care, and it is entirely unmemorable. When we meet someone new they say, "What do you do?" "Where are you from?" "Do you like films?" blah blah blah. We hate answering these questions over and over, yet we ask them of others. For attractive women who get approached regularly, it's even more of an issue.

Interviewing her

Many women are approached and immediately put on the spot to answer a series of questions. The man's only response to her answers is usually, "Oh really, so . . ." This quickly gets boring, and any woman who puts up with this for long must either be really attracted to you or very, very polite. Don't ask a series of questions. Ask one and connect on that point, then ask another. For advanced-level skills, try to elicit the answer without asking the boring question – make an assumption or guess about what she does, where she is from or what food she likes. You get the same information but it's more interesting for her.

Stating the obvious

If a girl has pretty eyes, she has probably been told that five hundred times. Find something more specific to her, preferably not about her appearance. Or don't compliment her at all. It's fine to give an obvious compliment with feeling when you're already together, but in the early stages it's not what she wants.

All the above methods of eliciting information may either put conversational pressure on the girl or else they're boring.

Hook elicitation

Here's what you should be doing instead. The following are some ways to elicit the standard information without asking boring questions.

Ask leading questions

Instead of asking, "Where are you from?" say, "Are you Swedish?" Make some kind of personal guess that shows you're paying attention to her.

Make assumptions and funny guesses

Instead of asking what she is doing, say, "Okay, so you're waiting to meet Steve, he is a guy you chatted up on the internet and you've no idea what he looks like, but he is going to be wearing a red shirt." She'll laugh, and then tell you what she is actually doing – or even better, she'll play along with it and you'll have a fun moment. Make up a silly scenario: What is she going to do with her friend? Why is she in London?

Another example would be: "Okay, so you've been shopping all day, bought loads of stuff and now your feet are killing you, so you're going for a coffee together." This kind of thing also gets you in the habit of focusing on women, making observations and cold reads. Over time, this skill develops and you can usually guess correctly!

Connecting on the hooks

After speaking to lots of girls about PUAT (lots work for me at our events), I have found out that they really don't get why men are scared about approaching them. They think that the men approaching them in these ways are naturally unfunny, uncharismatic, lack charm, have no confidence, etc. The thing is, the guy probably has lots of qualities, and he shows them to friends and family – people he is comfortable with. They don't understand that all of this goes out the window when an attractive female is in front of them. It took me a while to get to the point where I stopped worrying about how I was looking, how I was sounding, what I was going to say next, and was able to focus one hundred per cent on her. When this happened, I developed many of the theories and techniques you find here. One of the most important things that happens when you can focus on her is that you start using the hooks.

A 'hook' is something given to you that you can use to extend the interaction without starting a new, unrelated topic. Every time a woman opens her mouth she is giving you a hook. It might be her accent, the words she uses or the information she gives you. If she tells you she is Brazilian and studying English in London for three weeks, you have three hooks that you can feed off (Brazil, studying English, here for three weeks). The way to feed off a hook is to relate the point to them for a little while, which establishes a connection, and only then to ask another question or elicit another hook.

Your goal with each hook should be to connect in a positive way about the point. The best way to do this is to talk positively about her. The less effective way is to relate the point to your own experience, to be clichéd or negative. Let's look at the three levels of evolution in this area:

1. The high-pressure interview
You: "What do you do?"
Her: "I'm an artist."
You: "Cool, so . . . Where are you from?"
Her: "Switzerland."
You: "That's nice, what do you do in your spare time?"
Her: "I like going to the cinema."

Put yourself in the girl's position here. She is constantly under pressure, the spotlight is always on her and she is being asked to contribute a lot of information whilst getting nothing in return. Regardless of her answer, you are straight on to the next question. This is because you are thinking about the next question as she answers, instead of trying to use what she gives you in a unique way depending on her response. This is how most guys try to connect with girls.

2. Self-obsessed relating
You: "What do you do?"
Her: "I'm an artist."

You: "Cool, my brother is an artist, he makes these sculptures out of Plasticine, he made one the other day of a fish, it's really cool . . . . Where are you from?"
Her: "Switzerland."
You: "Oh great, I have a Swiss watch and I like Swiss chocolates. My friend went to Switzerland on holiday, said it was great. What do you do in your spare time?"
Her: "I like going to the cinema."
You: "Oh I love watching films, I saw that new Johnny Depp film, that was cool . . . I want to watch that new one coming out next week, forgot the name . . ."

What is going on here is that the person is using the hook, taking the pressure off the girl, so it's better than the interview. However, they are not making a connection, they are putting up a barrier. They are saying, "Anything you say I will relate to my reality and I won't try to understand yours." When someone is talking about themselves, it's less interesting than when they are talking about you. In this kind of conversation, the girl will not want to give more to the interaction because you have not shown empathy or understanding. At this level it takes a lot longer to get rapport and solid closes. Sure, it will work sometimes, especially if you have other talents that shine through when you're talking – humour being the one that can save the day. But to get fast rapport and connection, you need to do it like this:

3. Taking Things Deeper:

You: "What do you do?"

Her: "I'm an artist."

You: "Interesting, I like that, I imagine you must see the world in a different way to most people; you must be able to appreciate beauty in more things. Where are you from?"

Her: "Switzerland"

You: "You don't look like it, but I heard that people from Switzerland are quite conventional and really stick to rules and things. You look more like a bit of a rebel, just look at that hairstyle! What's a hobby of yours?"

Her: "I like watching films."

You: "I guess that, being a creative person, you must enjoy seeing other people's creativity. But when you look at art I guess you always see the technical aspects as well, so it must be nice to go to the cinema and just enjoy the experience."

The above are snippets from real conversations, but in the actual conversations I didn't jump around the topics in that way, because I was talking about her. It naturally flowed more deeply into those areas; because I was both making an attempt to understand her and to get things right, she opened up more, jumping in and expanding things, and the conversation got deep very quickly. By giving examples of the most boring questions possible and seeing how they become acceptable, you can see how this is a very powerful technique.

She would tell me more about her art, and natural questions arose from imagining what it was like to be her. If

I am imagining being an artist, I can talk generally about it, before wondering what kind of art. Then I'll ask her and have more information which I can use to imagine her more deeply, and so connect more deeply. This process continues usually until the topic naturally morphs into something else, rather than the staccato style in examples one and two.

Of course, you can relate things to yourself if they are particularly relevant and you have something interesting to say. But try to connect with her on the hook first, that way she'll be ten times more interested in what you have to say. It invokes the law of reciprocity – someone is interested in me, I'll be interested in them! If you purely talk about them, you'll even find that they sometimes have a little dialogue going on in their head that says, "Wow, this person is really great to talk to . . . Hang on! I don't know much about them," and then they start asking you loads of questions. When I connect I'm doing it by being empathetic, imagining what it's like to be her. I build up a picture, describe it and get more information to fill in the blanks.

Another kind of hook is an observational hook. This is something that you observe about her – her shopping bags, her clothes, her makeup, her nails, her body language, the expression on her face. These are all things you can use to create new conversational threads.

Attraction building – making her conversational threads more interesting

At some point she is going to want to contribute to the conversation and she will start to ask you questions. The danger here is that they are so super boring they kill any kind of interesting stuff you have going on. Here's how to be ready for this:

Have interesting answers to standard questions

There are certain questions and conversational paths that occur again and again for each person. Think about what yours are and make your input more interesting. If a conversation gets boring because the girl starts asking boring questions, she won't remember it was her fault – she'll just know she is bored! The obvious one is, "What do you do?" Either make your job interesting or describe it with passion; if it is dull, be brief and switch it to something more interesting, like a hobby – "But anyway, that's work, what I really like to do is . . ."

Stay away from topics like:

- Disgusting stuff.
- Religion.
- Contentious political issues.
- Violence.
- Bad past relationships.
- Negative things.

Talk with passion

If you can talk with passion about things you care about, it draws people in. If you enjoy something, let it show, be expressive, use visual and emotive language. People get caught up in it and start to feel good too. When they feel good, they will want to talk to you more. Use storytelling skills here.

So, let's put it all together with an example of the natural and situational observational opener. The following interaction was a real demonstration for a student. Location: Leicester Square, London, 3:30pm. I recorded it on MP3 and the transcript runs below. There are many techniques used which you can continue to refer to; you'll see more each time you look.

A girl stands alone with arms crossed, looking pretty unfriendly.

Me: Hi, you're crossing your arms and I study body language, so I could say that's because you're closed or in a bad mood; but I was noticing a lot of people standing like this recently, and either people are more closed at this time of year or more people are cold! [*laughs*] So are you in a bad mood or are you just cold?

Hot Chick: I'm cold.

(*I'm bantering without putting conversational pressure on her. This is necessary because I have no indication of interest and she looks unapproachable.*)

Me: See, people take this body-language stuff too seriously, they need to put more disclaimers in these books. People

119

crossing their arms are closed, *unless* they also might be cold. People stroking their hair fancy you, *unless* their hair is in their face and they can't see anything. [*laughs*] You look like you're waiting for someone?

HC: Yeah, I'm waiting for my friend.

(*At this point I don't immediately ask another question, like "Who?", "What time were they meant to be here?", "What are you doing together?" This would be natural but it's not very interesting. She has given me another hook which I can feed off, so I should use it. Her body language is opening up and she is receptive to the interaction.*)

Me: I hate waiting for people here, you can't call them because they are on the underground, and there are so many people so you keep thinking, "Is that them? Is that them?" The time goes way slower than when you're waiting somewhere less hectic. So let me guess, it's your old school friend and you're meeting for the ten-year reunion dinner?

HC: [*laughs*] Well, it's my friend from university but we are going for a coffee. What's your name?

(*This is a big sign of interest. She is asking a question of me. It isn't related to the topic and it's personal, which means she wants to know more about me and extend the interaction.*)

Me: Richard, and you?

HC: I'm Anna.

Both: Nice to meet you. [*shake hands*]

Me: Wow, your hands are cold. [*takes other hand too, squeezes them. I've quickly done a quite intimate thing that jumpstarts a* *sexual frame.*]

Me: So is your friend cute?

HC: [*laughs*] She is, actually.

Me: Cool, so we can all go for coffee together, but we can't stay long, we need to be somewhere. Tell her I'm your fiancé, that we met last week, it was a whirlwind romance, and that we flew to Vegas, got married by Elvis and came back yesterday.

[*laughs*]

Skills of the natural pretty much ended there, as we moved into a more two-way conversation and rapport. The interaction went on in a more relaxed style, she started giving fifty per cent of the conversation and asking a lot of questions. It wasn't as interesting because it didn't need to be. Her friend turned up (who was hot too) and we went for coffee together after persuading her friend it was cool. Number closed and ended the interaction after thirty minutes. Went to bed with her at the next meeting and she later became a girlfriend.

The key for the students on day game is this: there is no way to conversationally block an interaction unless she is being directly rude. Stay in there and learn something as you stretch yourself to come up with things to say; stay attentive to her and use the hooks.

EVOLUTION OF A NATURAL:
OCTOBER 2006

In October I held my first boot-camp. These are weekend-long events spanning twenty-four hours, and include a number of people paying hundreds of pounds each. My first one had six people. I was pretty stressed leading up to it. I'd listened to some advice on personal development which said, "Promise something you can't deliver and then move mountains to make it happen." I did certain things on one-on-ones, but for this I needed a different timetable because of the group dynamic. I planned improvisational acting exercises and had hired four girls for the students to practise on before we went to the club. This was a great idea and a key differentiator from other trainings. There was a girl Anthony P picked up in Stringfellows, her friend, my ex-girlfriend Rachel and a girl who I chatted up in the street. We paid them and luckily they all turned up on time. I was very nervous because I hadn't made public speeches before. However, I'd conditioned myself to embrace scary moments – I knew my fear meant I was going to learn a lot and that it would be great for my personal development. Another worry was the timing; I had no idea how long the exercises would take, or for how long we needed to talk about each subject. Amazingly, it went very smoothly; we had a great group of guys and they did very well. In the club later, they were getting numbers and kisses and all felt that they had learned a lot. Now the boot-camps are much better, they have been polished and refined, but the first one went off surprisingly without a hitch.

So far, I'd really liked two women since I moved to London, the Serbian girl and the French girl. They were both young and pretty, and I was sad when things went wrong. On a one-on-one in October, I was training in Trafalgar Square. I was getting the student to do some approaches when a very cute girl walked past, about five metres away; I waved and she waved back. For a minute or so I was debating whether to go after her or not. She slowed down as she typed a text message and so I ran after her. I told her exactly what I was thinking – that I wasn't going to run after her, but then she slowed right down and I just had to. I chatted about the National Gallery, why she wasn't at work in the daytime, and other small talk. Then I said I'd left my friend alone and should get back to him, but that we must meet up. Her name was Melissa. I took her number and tentatively set something up for two days later. The student was impressed and I was very happy to get such a fast number-close.

I called Melissa and we arranged to meet at night. We met at the station and I took her to a local bar. I didn't know that it was possible to have a date like this or to meet someone like her. She listened to what I had to say, and asked very penetrating questions which showed she was listening intently, really wanted to know more and was very intelligent. It's something I do too when I'm really interested in someone, and it was an amazing situation.

Within a couple of hours, we got to know each other at a deep level that really should have taken months. It turned out to be the best date I've ever had, and the most intense connection I've ever had with a girl.

She didn't like it in the bar, and I loved that she didn't like it. It was too noisy for her, and this was a great change from all the party girls who I meet in the night-time. It's why I believe that the daytime is when you meet girlfriend material. She obviously wanted to leave, and I asked if she wanted to come and have a bottle of wine at my house. We went back and I sat her down on the bed. So far we hadn't kissed, but the emotion in the air was incredible. It had been the perfect date, we were like soulmates. We were nodding at everything the other said, but it wasn't a fake kind of 'me too', it was genuine. We'd been together for about two hours and I decided it was time to kiss her; I moved closer, looked at her; she knew what was coming; I went in for the kiss. It was the most emotion-filled kiss I'd ever had; she felt it too. Afterwards she was crying, and I felt like doing the same!

We lay on the bed and kissed, and it was fantastic. She kissed my neck, shoulders and arms; it really turned me on. I had a girlfriend for two and a half years, and when she did this stuff it did nothing for me. I know that girls do to you the kind of things that they like done to themselves, but this was the first time I'd enjoyed anything like this.

She wanted to go and get the last tube, and this was

where I made my first mistake; I persuaded her to stay longer and she missed it. She felt a bit uncomfortable because she didn't want to sleep with me on the first date, and she didn't have all her toiletries. Still, she committed to staying the night; I was happy about that. We were kissing and things were heating up, but she stopped me as I went to take her knickers off and told me she had her period. She said she wished that she didn't have to tell me that, and that I hadn't pushed for sex so soon.

In the morning I went to get breakfast from a patisserie; it was very nice, and I saw her off at the tube station. She told me there was a party the next day; she was going with her friends and invited me along. But I had a boot-camp the day after the party, so I didn't think I'd come. I called her on the night of the party and found out it was just around the corner from my house, so I decided to pop over there for a while.

I pre-planned things because I wanted everything to be perfect. Firstly, I had messed up with the Serbian girl by always being around and not leaving until she had to go somewhere else. I planned to go for strictly half an hour and then leave. Secondly, I'd had a problem with my ex-girlfriend's friends, who all disliked me. I just wasn't very good socially. I didn't have anything to say to them and basically just took my girlfriend away any time I came around, so eventually I got on their nerves. So I was going to go in there and wow Melissa's friends with my new social skills. I was listening to music and pretty pumped up because I was excited to see her, and also because I had a boot-camp coming up the next day.

I jogged down to the party, and found my way to her. I saw her friends and switched on my extrovert character, being Mr. Sociable, bantering, etc. They liked me and were smiling and laughing. I spent some time chatting with Melissa, then kissed her and went back home. I told her about my event at the weekend and that I'd call her on Monday.

It was lucky that we had our telephone conversation on Monday and not Saturday, or else it would have ruined the boot-camp! She told me that she felt weird because I'd been a completely different person at the party. She thought she knew me so well, and then she had met someone completely different and was very confused. She also told me that she wanted to meet again, to see what was going on. When I met her, Melissa resisted when I went to kiss her; she said that, while she was confused, she wanted to take it easy and wait. It created a very weird dynamic, I felt uncomfortable and so did she. It wasn't a great meeting. I had messed up by not being completely myself in the one situation when I could have been.

We met once more and there was the same awkwardness. Afterwards her dad came to visit, so she was busy, then she went back to Spain for a week. We talked on the phone but didn't meet, and after a couple of weeks she didn't return my calls.

MISSION SIX

Practise your new conversation skills on your social circle. See if you can make them feel good and get a deeper level of connection than you normally do. You'll notice that you get a much better reaction from people and can even use these skills at work.

THE HOOK POINT AND INDICATORS OF INTEREST

The hook point is when a girl shows interest in extending the interaction. She is happy for you to stick around and talk more. You can tell you've reached the hook point when:

- She asks you questions.
- She asks your name.
- She gives extended answers to your questions.
- Her body language changes and becomes more open.

Once you've reached the hook point, you should look for indicators of sexual interest.

If she is sexually attracted to you:

- She strokes her neck when in conversation with you.
- She looks at your mouth.
- She tilts her head to the side when speaking to you.
- Her pupils dilate.
- She laughs too much at your jokes, even when they aren't funny.

- She is happy listening to you, even when you're talking rubbish.
- She holds eye contact with you and doesn't look around the room, or at her friends. Note: if she is nervous, and it's just not in her character to hold strong eye contact, she could still be interested.
- She is comfortable with you touching her and invading her space.
- She shows willingness to leave her friends and stay with you.
- She laughs and hits you on the shoulder when you tease her.
- She looks at you in a dreamy kind of way.
- She asks if you're single.
- She is comfortable with pauses in the conversation.
- She says your name in conversation.
- She leans into you.

RAPPORT

In 'Skills of the Natural', I talked about how to make connections with the girl. This continues now in the rapport phase. The difference is that the goal here has become to find a reason to see her again, and to discover mutual interests. You know the process of connecting, but how do you elicit the desired result?

1. Be observant

Notice things about her appearance (clothes, accessories, hair, nails, jewellery). Women usually put a lot of time and effort into the way they look; her bag might be chosen to match her shoes, belt, earrings and dress. Most people don't notice, so she will be happy if you do. Jewellery and accessories also often have a story behind them, or may mean something to the girl.

2. Talk about things that evoke passion and feeling

What is she very passionate about? It might be anything from friends and family to travel or ballet. Connect on these points by showing you understand why she feels that way.

RAPPORT AND COMFORT-BUILDING QUESTIONS

I've told you to avoid asking the usual boring questions. So what kind of things would it be okay to ask? The best questions build comfort and create a connection that elicits emotion. The following offer some good examples:

Do you remember your first day at school?
This is something that she probably won't have talked about for a long time, but it has strong emotions attached to it. It can also age-regress the girl (a hypnosis term). Do not be surprised if she suddenly starts acting very childishly. To ask a question like this, you can't just say,

"Where are you from? What do you do? Do you remember your first day at school?" The first thing you need to do is to root the question. This means that you need to lead into it smoothly. You could do this by saying, "You know, I was walking down the street this morning and I passed a bakery and smelled the freshly baked apple pie. It immediately took me back to when I was six years old, and I spent the next thirty minutes walking around like a kid with a silly expression on my face because I was remembering my childhood so vividly. What about you, do you remember your first day at school?" Any question like this should be rooted correctly, and there are many ways to do that. After she has given her response, you should connect on it. You could say, "I can just imagine you with your My Little Pony lunchbox, skipping to school." Next, you should relate your own story. If you can connect like this on a few emotional topics, then you've built a deep connection in a short amount of time. You'll already have talked about stuff that's not normally talked about until you've dated a girl for three months or so.

If you could wake up tomorrow anywhere in the world, where would it be?

This is another good question, and replaces boring questions such as "Do you like travel?" and "Did you go on holiday this year?" This one doesn't need so much rooting; it could simply be, "I need a holiday – let me ask you, if you could wake up anywhere in the world tomorrow, where would it be?" Connect on her answer – "Yeah, lying on the beach, with the sun beating down, the sound of the ocean . . ." – then relate your own in vivid detail. This is a good one for trance-state visualisation, evoking feelings of comfort and relaxation which she'll later relate to being with you.

Are your friends mostly men or women?
This tells you something about her character and also gets her talking about people she cares about.

What's the one thing you can't say no to?
This is a good way to find out something she really enjoys. It could be chocolate. Perhaps fresh orange juice. It should make her eyes light up. You can then describe how good it is to eat that chocolate, how it feels when you put it in your mouth and taste it as it melts. Do this and watch how you can lead her into a desiring state.

What talents do you have that would surprise me?
This is a great question and a challenge. Early on in an interaction, she won't feel any need to answer challenging questions. By the rapport stage, she will feel some pressure to respond to a question like this to prove herself to you. Remember that she is likely to ask the same back to you, so have something ready.

Have you ever been in love?

Root it, and dig a bit deeper about the times she has been in love. Don't ask what happened – this would focus on the break-up! Make her want those feelings again; since she is with a cool guy, she'll probably be imagining them with you. This is a great one for a number of reasons: firstly, it brings out the emotion and memories connected with love; secondly, it starts her imagining a relationship with you.

Think of your own questions too, and follow the process of:

- Rooting.
- Asking.
- Connecting.
- Answering.

When you've done this, you'll already have a deep connection with the girl. On numerous occasions, girls have told me after just a few hours that they feel like they have known me for three months. The reason is:

- I am completely comfortable, open and relaxed with them.
- I am making them as comfortable as they normally feel after three months.
- They are feeling things that they would normally only feel within a committed relationship.
- They are talking about things they would only normally talk about with very close friends, family or the long-term boyfriend.

EVOLUTION OF A NATURAL: NOVEMBER 2006

Decided to blow off voice training and a date this night, and instead went to the World Music Awards in Earls Court. I got two tickets from a friend of mine who knows very high-up music executives. I'm getting some good connections so I'm getting invited to better parties. Arrived at 6pm with my journalist friend and breezed in with my red-level band, which gave me access to the internal red carpet. Aside from security there were maybe ten people on the red carpet, and we mingled with the stars as they arrived. Journalists and paparazzi were behind a barrier. Saw Jordan and Peter Andre, Eva Herzigova, Paris Hilton, Victoria Silvstedt, Natalie Imbruglia, plus a bunch of people I don't recognise but who paparazzi were snapping like crazy.

Backstage dressing rooms. Most of these women were mingers up close; the hottest girl I saw aside from Paris Hilton was working there as a waitress. I shot some good video too on the red carpet. Paris was one of the last to arrive, and we breezed into the celebrity dressing-room area with her entourage. As I always say, "Do anything with enough authority . . ." Nelly Furtado, Beyonce, Rihanna, Chris Brown, etc. all had their little trailer things and everyone else in there had staff bands or performer bands. Pretty funny.

Not thinking PU at all at the moment. Next I got in with Beyonce's entourage as she went on stage, and got in the wings with the crew. Beyonce is stressed so I save the

133

'dye hair blond' opener for later. I could have run onstage and done a little dance and grabbed the mike, but was persuaded not to by friend. Journalist friend took camera at this point and went to snap Michael Jackson, Beyoncé, etc. I was watching the performers standing nervously before they went on.

Some dancers were preparing to go onstage and I saw a cute one, approached with pretty standard chat (although was doing ninety per cent of the talking to start), but made a little connection. Paced and led into calm voice because she was nervous, it calmed her down, so I guess that's NLP in action. When she came back out, I got her number and more importantly got her to give me her gold-level wristband, which is for performers. Line: "Hey, gimme your wristband because you've finished." Walked back to VIP and briefly stopped by area near stage where tables are £8k each to watch the show. These guys don't get closer than twenty metres to anyone and it's a bit lame. Get some food and then back into the VIP area.

Meet Katie Melua, watch Eva Herzigova dance like a nutter with her crew. Chatted to the two girls I met on the red carpet again and found out where the fake after-party is at – they are going to the club Paper. There is a secret one, I ask Katie Melua, it's at number one Dover St – Mahiki, "See you there, Katie," she flaked. We leave and go on the tube, forgetting our VIP lifestyle for a half-hour. And arrive at the club where I use my secret "get in when not on guest list" routine. I can't give this out to anyone, as no one knows it.

It works, and we are inside this club now with Paris Hilton, Lindsay Lohan, Roberto Cavalli, Rachel Hunter, Sting, and whoever else. There is no VIP, this is intimate, we are the only people who aren't *somebody*. Free bar, I get drunk. Work the room a little bit, lots of beautiful girls. I identify two solid eights. Elle 'the Body' MacPherson turns up, and I can see that she would be serious competition for Paris as the hottest celebrity in the place if she were ten years younger – she's forty-one, I think. When they meet I open them both with, "Have you ever taken a picture together?" They pose for a couple for me and then get me to take one with their camera. I tell Paris that she'd be lucky to look like Elle when she is over forty. She is actually really chilled and agrees.

For forty-one, she is damn hot. Paris then dances like a nutter for a bit. I chat to her friend who has Marilyn Monroe hairstyle. Dunno who the hell it is. She is a bit funny looking due to collagen lips, etc. Paris's bodyguard is cool with me now and doesn't watch me when I am close to her. I open my target for the night, a tall blonde Italian. I think she is second hottest in the club after Paris. She's just watched me with Paris and her friend, so I open with, "Hey, how's it going?" She's standing there arms crossed. I ask if she is working security, she says no; I make her laugh by saying she had that killer look for a second and looked like she could do some crazy flying kick if anyone messed with Paris. Excuse to check out shoes, touch her up a bit.

I make her laugh with my spontaneous bullshit. She is a little drunk, I am too. I do my salsa kino-escalation. Touch her hair. Two-minute kiss-close without knowing her name. Club empties out as I hang out with her, get some rapport and connection but I'm basically in seduction mode because we are drunk anyhow. She is something to do with Roberto Cavalli. There are less than fifteen people left in the club. We hang out with Paris, the staff and her entourage.

By now, Paris is very cool. At the awards she was pretending she was on the phone and didn't talk to the press, now she is relaxed and open with everyone. I number close, but only the club owner. My camera is full, I can't delete any pics because they are worth money, and journalist friend takes camera and leaves to go and write stories and sell pics. Italian girl and I hang out. Paris goes to another party at Boujis (at 2.30!). I get a peck on the cheek

I say to my girl that we should go somewhere else too. Lead her outside, get taxi to my place. She asks, when we are going through the door to my house, where the hell we are. I say I'm going to show her where I live and then change the subject. Take her to my room, sit her on my bed. No need for wine. She is probably hottest girl I ever had in there. I'm completely calm due to mix of what happened that day and alcohol. I chat with her, kiss her, slowly and smoothly work things up. She is super hot, best-looking girl I'd ever slept with, and a great way to end a fantastic night at a celebrity event and after-party. Silver Cavalli dress is on the floor of my rented room.

She had to rush out early to work (still don't know exactly what she does). She is going back to Italy the next day but I get her email.

MISSION SEVEN

Open sets, get past the hook point and use a couple of the above questions and follow the process of getting a connection.

Using Hooks and Connecting

When you find out something about the person, it's a hook that you should try to use: where they are from; where they went on holiday; a passion; an interest; something with emotional content; a future dream. You want to connect with it in a positive way. There are seven ways to deal with a hook. Let's use the example of discovering the person wants to go to New York: "I'd really love to go to New York. I've never been there." The seven ways this can be dealt with are:

1. "Cool, I'd like to go to Barbados," OR "Oooh, New York? I don't like big cities [*rejection, BAD*]."
2. "Yeah, me too [*try-hard connecting, BAD*]."
3. "Cool, my brother just got back from there [*semi-rejection relating to self, NEUTRAL*]."

4. "Cool, the shopping is great and you can go watch a Broadway show [*positive logical connection, OKAY*]."
5. "Oooh, the people there are supposed to be rude and it's very busy and crowded [*negative logical connection, BAD*]."
6. "Wow, New York. So you can walk around and imagine you're on a movie set, with the yellow cabs, the hustle and bustle, the lights in Times Square and a stroll through Central Park. That's a great holiday [*positive connection, affirming their choice with visualisation, emotional connection, GOOD*]."
7. "Yeah, you seem like that kind of person, I think you'd love the energy there, you'll feel right at home in the busy streets, people watching, taking things in [*purely emotional connecting, cold-reading, GOOD*]."

This is a very powerful tool for making a connection. You are making her feel good about herself and her interests and you are showing understanding of them. The dynamite comes later in deep rapport.

EVOLUTION OF A NATURAL: NOVEMBER 2006

My friend Anthony P is a big fan of strip clubs. He likes them because the girls are hot, they are sexual and they approach you. I went a few times with him; prior to this, I'd only been to Stringfellows once with my first girlfriend. I had a good time but spent lots of money and never imagined that it was possible to actually pick up these girls. After going a few times, I realised that it was not only possible but not *that* difficult. They work unsocial hours and don't meet many people, so if you ask most of them where they meet their boyfriends they'll tell you that it's inside the clubs.

One day, Anthony P invited me to Secrets strip club; I'd been to a few others and was able to connect with some girls, but hadn't got any closes. I was pretty confident by this time at student parties and regular bars, and was getting used to high-class venues. So here we were at Secrets in Euston. I got into a conversation with a very attractive brunette from Russia. She'd been in England a while, and we got on very well very quickly, we had very compatible personalities. About twenty minutes in, though, I realised something was wrong. I know she found me attractive (she verbalised this), but she wouldn't consider me as anything more than a friend. I could tell that she wasn't sexually interested because of the way she looked at me, there just wasn't any sexual tension. She was very confident and very sexual, talking about sex and what kind of man she wanted. Then I said, "You like me, but you know I can't handle you sexually, don't you?" She said that was exactly it. Basically I could handle a student girl, a nice girl, a quiet girl, but I couldn't handle a very sexually confident girl that wanted a very manly man. I just hadn't slept with enough girls and wasn't confident enough to deal with her. She could see that. This was when I first realised the importance of sexual confidence. If you have the belief that you can deal with a very strong and sexual woman, and you project this belief, then you will be able to attract all types of women. Subconsciously, many women want a man who can dominate them sexually. At this point, I probably couldn't have handled her! My friend Cardenas, who teaches sexual confidence and some sexual techniques for PUATraining and Master Your Sex Life, had told me that I choose very nice girls, good girls. He likes 'filthy' girls, and is quite extreme sexually – he teaches technique to guys on weekend courses using live demonstrations! However, he was right about me and why I probably couldn't handle the overtly sexual girls.

I left the club having had an amazing connection with her, but failing to get a number because of this. I decided that this was another piece of the puzzle that I hadn't assembled yet.

ISOLATING

To close a girl, in most cases, you need to isolate her. Have you ever noticed that conversations with large groups are very lightly topical, compared to a one-on-one interaction where it can go very deep? Which conversation is more likely to bring out emotions, to help you get to know someone better and form a bond? That's why we need to isolate.

My definition of isolation is not that you're the only people in the location, but that the two of you are the only people in the conversation. Her friends could be one metre away, as long as they are not involved. For me, the easiest way to isolate a girl is to turn her away from her group. She doesn't need to leave them completely and walk away with you, just as long as she isn't looking at them. A student once asked me to open a girl who was part of a group of six. I might have opened the whole group, bantered for a while, won them over and then tried to isolate her from there. But there are two reasons why I don't like doing this.

Firstly, I don't always want to bust out enough energy to entertain a huge group in a noisy location. Secondly, my problem in the past has been that if I show too much lack of interest to the group they all want to talk to me, and isolating one girl becomes difficult – she feels social pressure as well because all eyes are on her.

So I wanted to come up with a way to isolate her 'under the radar'. What I did in this case was notice that the group had pretty much split in half. I approached, quickly established physical contact (I turned her around by the shoulder before saying a word), introduced myself and – lo and behold – we were isolated as she turned away from her two friends.

With a pair of girls, isolation is very difficult. Generally speaking, you need a wing in this situation. For a group of three, my simple isolation strategy would be to open everyone, reach the hook point and then deliver a personal statement to the girl I like (example: observation about her jewellery). The key here is to speak at a lower volume and break eye contact with the others. They should engage each other. The eye contact and attention you're paying the target should ensure she continues it with you. You next sidestep slightly around the target and away from the obstacles, so she has to turn to face you. You're now isolated. Wasn't that easy?

Leading to Isolate

You generally want to be leading the girl at all times. "Let's go dance," "let's sit down," "let's go get a drink" are all ways to lead and isolate. Others include "come over into the light" – to do a proper palm reading, and see her eye colour – or "Let's go over there, it's less crowded/noisy/smoky."

DEEP RAPPORT

Use this technique with caution. I call the closes I can get with this 'GF-closes', girlfriend closes. I can almost make a girl fall in love with me using my rapport skills. I am careful to only do this with girls I genuinely feel something for. It's immoral to use it on those I would only consider for a casual relationship. Deep rapport is a way to get a soulmate-level connection with the girl and go beyond anything she has ever felt before. It's a simple two-stage process. Once mastered, it can be done on the fly with any girl. The steps are:

1. Elicit emotional content.
2. Feedback and connect.

First I'll explain the process and then give an example.

These subjects have emotions attached to them:
- Passions and interests.
- Memories (e.g. childhood).
- Future ambitions and dreams.
- People close to us.

Let's use the example of passions, but remember it applies to all of the above. Your goal should be to get down to this deep emotional level and connect. Every person has things they are passionate about. These aren't critical 'must do' activities, but provide a sense of joy, achievement or 'being alive'.

Some examples could be:
- Dancing.
- Theatre.
- Museums.
- Art.
- Playing an instrument.
- Reading fiction.
- Fishing.
- Golf.
- Poetry.
- Collecting something.

These all share common elements. They are ways that the person chooses to spend their time – you have passions, I have passions, and the girls you meet will have passions. Let's look at the typical ways they are dealt with in conversation:

Girl: Actually I do ballet, I've done it for ten years.

Guy: Cool, you must be very flexible.

Or

Guy: Cool, I saw *Swan Lake*.

Or

Guy: Oh, my mum made me do it when I was a kid, I hated it.

Or

Guy: I'd like to see you in your tutu.

Or

Guy: Me too.

Or

Guy: Cool, I like football.

Or

Mystery Method Guy: Oh my God, I can't talk to you any more. You're a ballet dancer? Oh my God, this girl at school was a ballet dancer and she bullied me . . .

This pretty much covers all the possible responses to ballet or any other passion. Let's think about this for a second. The girl has revealed to you something that she is very passionate about. She has done it for ten years, purely out of a personal sense of commitment. In the above examples, her offer to you has been rejected. You might as well have asked if she likes oranges, because you've treated her passion in a superficial way. If you're going to do this, you might as well stay on superficial subjects.

Don't dismiss her passion in any of the above ways.

Connect with her on it. You could lie and say how much you love ballet. I don't like to lie, so I wouldn't do this. What you *can* do is be empathetic. Imagine why she loves ballet, what she feels when she dances. I show that I understand why she loves ballet without saying that I love it. It's something she has never heard before and it establishes the soulmate connection. My answer would be made up on the spot following the guideline of seeking to empathise as to why she might love ballet:

"Wow, that's so cool, you must be very dedicated to have kept it up for ten years, I mean when you're young it's easy, but as you get older you get more and more commitments." (This is a standard connection for any long-term committed passion.)

"So you must really love dancing. Most people have their nine-to-five jobs and come home and watch TV. It's refreshing to find someone with a passion that's expressive and artistic." (This is standard for any artistic or creative passion.)

"People might think that dancing is just learning steps and performing them, but I think that dance is something that brings out the soul in someone; you can dance robotically by perfectly learning the steps, but it's when you really feel them that you become great. I also imagine that it's a way of expressing your feelings through the movement of your body, like an artist does on canvas or a musician does through their instrument. When you're in the moment, you're expressing yourself through the way you move. It must go back to before we communicated with speech and used dance and ritual to express our emotions. I'd love to see you perform."

Now you can see why this is so powerful. It can be applied to any passion, whether you empathise with it or not. Examples:

Fishing is about being with nature, serenity (being alone with your thoughts) mixed with anticipation, mixed with excitement, when you catch something.

Stamp collecting is about a sense of achievement. Each stamp has a memory attached because it's from a different time in your life. Your stamp book is like a book of memories.

Going out and getting drunk on a Friday night is about how you've been stressed at work all week, and that moment when you're with your friends, have been drinking and are just completely in the moment. Just feeling the enjoyment without a care in the world. That sense of release from it all.

EVOLUTION OF A NATURAL: DECEMBER 2006

December for me is all about one night. It was one of the most memorable nights of my life, and in some ways it was bad that it happened. I must say that, if I weren't teaching guys how to be better with women, I probably would have stopped trying to progress around September time, when I could get numbers and dates pretty easily with girls that I was attracted to. Because I've kept getting better, because I have an obligation to my customers, I have pushed the boundaries, which makes it harder for me to settle down and choose just one girl. My standards have got higher and higher and I've met girls with extremely good looks, high intelligence and appealing personalities, which means it will be harder to be satisfied.

One night in December I went to the 24 club on Kingly Street for a party organised by the website Beautiful People Network. The 'beautiful people' weren't especially beautiful and definitely weren't very interesting, but we had some free cocktails and the club later opened up to the normal crowd. I was dancing and having fun, and a few girls were dancing near me in a way that I have come to learn means 'we like you'. I danced with them and created some social proof. A girl then walked through the crowd towards me and I made sexual eye contact. She got closer, I blocked her path, she looked at me, I slowly went in and kissed her. Kissing a girl within a few seconds is an advanced skill; it is basically engaging that sexual state straight away and testing whether they are comfortable with it. It requires complete confidence. We kiss, she takes a picture with me, then goes to rejoin her friends. After she goes, some other girls begin to fight for my attention; I've managed to create some social proof and am suddenly the highest-value guy in the club, even though I'm not buying champagne and don't have a Ferrari. Girls start approaching me, inviting me to parties and asking for my number. I'm not especially attracted to any of them and have had fun already, so I leave with Anthony P.

This is a good point at which to talk about state. Everyone who I know who is great with women has nights when they are just on a roll, where they feel on top of the world and can approach any girl with no possibility of getting rejected. I got into this state that night and was still in it as I walked home. It was raining as we were walking down Shaftesbury Avenue back to Covent Garden. I was talking to Anthony P when he suddenly looked like he'd seen a ghost. He told me, "There is an incredibly beautiful girl over there." She was under a shelter, trying to keep out of the rain. She was stunning. I only saw one other girl as hot as her that year, and that was in Riga, Latvia. She was hotter than Paris Hilton and whoever else attended those celeb parties. Blonde, as tall as me with heels, perfect skin, green/blue eyes, slim, toned, elegant, perfect ass and boobs. I wouldn't have changed anything.

I stood a couple of metres away, mirroring the look on her face in a funny way. I had my leather jacket under my top because it was raining; she looked at it quizzically and I mimed that it was my baby. I looked at the shelter; there wasn't enough room for me until she took a step back to make some space, and I went to stand next to her. I made small talk but I was in seduction mode, looking at her like I wanted her. I went for the kiss within twenty seconds, but she turned her face so I kissed her on the cheek. In my experience this isn't a rejection, it's just that they don't want to make it too easy. I asked her where she was going, told her she was heading the wrong way and started walking her in the rain towards my house! I asked if she wanted to go somewhere else for a drink. She said yes. I took her to my front door and then she physically and verbally dissented. She said I was a prick and that I thought all Russian girls were easy. I said sincerely, because I meant it, "No. I love Russian girls, and they are very classy." She physically showed her objection had gone, so I led her into my place and took her to my room. She sat on the windowsill, looking so damn sexy. I went up, got in her face but didn't kiss her. There was tons of sexual tension. I teased her for a bit, then we kissed. I pulled her to standing position, and then tripped her up on to the bed. She gave no last-minute resistance, took her clothes off, and she was just incredible looking. The sex was great, just because it was such an exciting situation with a jaw-droppingly beautiful girl.

She had a boyfriend, was very rich (£5k earrings) and was going back home for the holidays. If I had a picture of her, I could just put it on the sign-up page of the website and I'd get twice as many customers! She was that hot. She had to leave at 6am to get back, otherwise "the security guards will tell my dad." I didn't get enough of a connection because her English was not good enough. I wanted to stay in bed with her and just look at her some more.

One of my lasting memories is that, when she was

getting dressed again, she asked what I did and I talked about what I teach. I mentioned body language. She did a sexy dance, wiggled her ass and said, "How is my body language?" *Wow!*

I had flashbacks for the next few days because she was just too damn hot. A week later I was talking about her with two friends, walked out into the middle of the road and nearly got killed. It took me a few weeks to get back to finding other girls attractive again. I've tasted forbidden fruit. After that night, my mission became even tougher. I won't be one hundred per cent happy until I have a girl as hot as her, but with the personality of Melissa.

KINO-ESCALATION

This was my sticking point for a while. I missed the whole thing where people started hugging when they met. I didn't get the whole double-cheek-kiss thing. I wasn't comfortable touching people. But the fact is, most people like to be touched. Hugs feel good. Someone touching your arm when they offer their emotional support feels better. A lot of guys have problems with touching because they are scared of being perceived as creepy. Yes, women hate being grabbed by the drunk guys at the bar, but if they are talking to someone that they like they want to be touched by them!

Kino-escalation is the process of going all the way from

incidental touches to sex. Obviously the first time you touch a girl generally can't be when you kiss her; that'd be weird. You need to get her comfortable with your touching, and there are lots of ways to do this. Some key points on kino:

- Intent: Women can sense the intent behind kino. An arm on the shoulder from someone thinking, "Okay, now I'm going to escalate by putting my arm on her shoulder," will make her feel weird. She'll subconsciously know the difference between creepy touching and nice touching because she has been touched by a lot of men! The average woman has been touched by eighteen thousand, four hundred and seventy-two men in her life.* When she is attracted to you, you can get away with anything you like, but until that point the intent should be pure. When *you* touch her, make it part of your natural movements, touch her in the same way you would touch a friend and keep the intent behind it positive and natural. Don't think sleazy thoughts! When you have attraction, you can have a sexual intent behind your kino that will be completely cool.

- Speed: The faster the kino, the more you can get away with, because it becomes harder to object to. The brain doesn't have time to register the hand on the shoulder if it's just there for a second. If you gesture a lot, build

---

* I love making up statistics!

in some rapid kino and it will allow you to escalate more quickly and smoothly than usual.

• Eye contact: Do not look at the part of her that you're touching, it draws attention and feels 'icky' to women. When you go to escalate kino in a major way, maybe by putting your arm around her, eye contact will make it an intensely high-pressure moment. If you're looking away when you make this move, it's much more comfortable and acceptable. Use the looking-away trick when taking her hand, or anything else that seems too intimate at the time.

Excuses to touch

During an approach I did the other day, I used some methods I made up on the spot to advance kino leading up to a kiss close. I normally date girls a few years younger than me, and was genuinely surprised to find a girl my age (twenty-six) who looked really young. I said, "You must use good moisturiser," and stroked her face with the back of my index finger. If she flinched in the slightest, the kiss close wouldn't have been on. I also touched her hair and asked if she ever wore it up. The kiss was on at this point, and we both knew it. I did a couple of things to dial up the tension even more, then finally kissed her. I'm still wondering about whether there is any benefit to delaying the kiss to build more tension, as opposed to going for it as soon as it's on. Having excuses to touch solves the problem of kino-escalation for anyone not used to touching strangers in conversation. Below are some ways to kino-escalate:

- Don't shake her hand when introduced, hold it for about three seconds. It's long enough to notice, but not long enough to object to.
- Use high-fives when you find something cool about her.
- If she goes to the gym, exercises, looks tough or whatever, it's an excuse to feel her muscles. Flex your arm and point at her to do the same.
- Check out her jewellery. Hold her hand to see her rings or bracelets. Move her hair back to check out her earrings. You can use many excuses to check out her hair. "Ever wear it up?" "Is that your natural colour?" "Ever had it long/short?"
- Take her pulse.
- Ask if she salsas, or does any other dance, and dance with her. Don't ask if she wants to, just lead.
- If she gives you any shit, you can take her hand, put it on your chest and say, "Oh, you're breaking my heart!"
- Palmistry.
- Arm-in-arm leading.
- Teasing – poking, prodding, tickling, play-fighting, barging, nudging – all great playful ways to kino-escalate.

Sexual escalation techniques

There are more of these in the 'Sexual Spikes' subsection. These are purely physical (the others are verbal, or a combination of both):

- Finger playing: when you're holding hands, play with her fingers and see if she reciprocates: this is surprisingly sexy and a great test.
- Hand Squeeze: squeeze her hand and see if she squeezes back. This is a great indicator that the kiss close is definitely on.
- Triangular gazing: this is a method of making her think in a sexual way. Look at her left eye, then the right, then the lips. One second on each. Repeat.
- Slow blink: blink slowly; this is very sexy.

Playful escalation and sexual escalation

You can escalate kino in two ways, sexually and playfully. The best way to escalate with a friend or a girl from your social circle is to playfully test out her receptiveness, instead of making a high-pressure move to sexually escalate. Sexual escalation has a sexual intent behind it. Playful escalation seems more safe to them because it's what brothers and sisters do. But it's also what boyfriends and girlfriends in a comfortable relationship do, so it's a great way to escalate and trigger enjoyable feelings of sexual tension.

Kino-escalation process

All of these steps can sometimes be skipped and you can go straight for a kiss. It might work sometimes. But to smoothly lead into it, you're ramping up the kino bit by bit. The process below is a smooth path from nothing to kissing. You can also combine it with some verbal sexual escalation (see 'Sexual Spikes'):

- Touch shoulder.
- Take hand (use excuse).
- Dance.
- Hold hand.
- Squeeze hand.
- Touch hair (use excuse).
- Touch face.
- Kiss.

Closing

NUMBER CLOSING

GOING FOR A NUMBER IS A HIGH-PRESSURE MOMENT FOR MOST GUYS — THEY DON'T KNOW WHEN TO DO IT, AND THEY DON'T KNOW WHETHER THE GIRL WILL ACCEPT OR REJECT THEM. Even after getting a number, it can be difficult to convert it into a date or another meeting. I used to have pretty good conversations and then not ask for the number, either because I'd feel bad about revealing that it was indeed a pick-up attempt, or I'd be afraid she'd say no. I figured out that it becomes easy if you do it smoothly. Here's what to do!

Conversation leading to a number close

Most guys make the mistake of making small talk for a period of time and then just coming out and asking for a number. This is wrong. A connection can be (but usually isn't) built on small talk, but it takes a lot longer. Instead, the conversation needs to be directed towards the goal at all times. A conversation aimed at getting a number needs to be based around connections and common interests:

- What does she do when she isn't working? How does she spend her time?
- What food does she like? What places does she like to go to in the evening? Is she a party girl? Does she like the arts? Is there something she would like to do but hasn't yet (e.g. salsa class)?

These are basic common interest questions that lead to a possible connection. Think of your own; there are hundreds of possible permutations. Taking two opposite examples, let me show you how to lead into a number close from a general conversation:

You: What places do you like to go in the evening?
Her: I like club/bar X.
You: Cool, it's good there. Have you ever been to club Y?
Her: Yeah/no.
You: Well, me and some friends are going there on X day, you should come.
Her: Yeah/okay.
You: Excellent. What's your number?
Or
You: What do you like to do when you're not working?

Her: I like to go to the theatre/exhibitions/museums/ballet.

You: Have you been to that new show/exhibition/whatever?

Her: No.

You: Me neither, we should go.

Her: Okay sure.

You: Great, give me your number.

(*You never ask for a number directly, it should flow naturally. The close should be assumed.*)

How about if you can't find a connection, don't have time to, or for some other reason just don't have a conversation like the above? You can use the universal:

You: You're cool/It's interesting talking to you, we should hang out.

Her: Yeah.

You: [*hands her the phone*] What are you doing on Thursday?

Finally, most guys get numbers that flake. So minimise flakeage:

Enter your number in her phone too. Have a connection or something you can do together, as described above. And most importantly, arrange a date there and then. If you've already arranged a date, she can be thinking about it when you call. Apply these tips and all your good interactions should end in solid number closes.

Now is a good time to mention dealing with future

objections. This subject is almost big enough to warrant its own section, so pay attention! The situation: She is tipsy, you meet in a bar, you have a great time. Easy to see her again? Not always. The problem is, she is going to go home, talk to her friends and be distracted by all the other guys chasing her. You can easily turn into "the dude I met when I was drunk", even though you might have made the most incredible connection of all time. You can be thinking she'll fall in love with you, but she'll flake! The way you deal with this is by making statements that put the potential objection out there before she thinks of it later:

"I know we are drunk, but I can tell that we'll get along great. It'll be excellent to meet up somewhere more quiet and really get to know each other."

"I can't believe we've met in a club, I didn't expect to meet a great girl in a nightclub. We might go home and think that it was just an amazing connection because of the environment. That might be the case, but I'd love to find out by getting to know you better in a more chilled-out location."

By doing this, she can remain focused on meeting you again and not dwell on the potential problems. This is especially important if you escalated kino pretty hard; you'll also have to deal with: "Maybe he's a player," and "If we meet again, he'll be all over me straight away." You can use the same method to deal with these issues too.

159

EVOLUTION OF A NATURAL: JANUARY 2007

Business was good; my personal life was good; I was very happy. In some ways, it must be similar to winning the lottery. My life had changed overnight. People just assumed that I'd always been good socially, had women and been happy and positive. On my weekend events, I had to show one of my old student-card pictures, otherwise guys would just tell me that it was easy for me because I was good looking and socially confident! I'd engineered the person and the life that I wanted. But I still had loads to learn.

On a night in early January, I went out with no idea of where I was going, we just wandered around and tried to find somewhere new and interesting. All we found were boring places, but, on leaving one of them, the following scene took place . . .

Transcript

Situation: Friday night, leaving a bar at 10pm with one friend. We leave because there are no hot babes. I hear another door opening behind me as I walk along the street and see one gorgeous Italian and her less attractive friend from Croatia come out of the same bar we were in. How we didn't see them inside, I don't know. I let them catch up, walk in step as if we are together and then say:

Richard: So where are we going now? Because that place was pretty lame.

Croatia: I don't know.

Richard: There's a place over there that's pretty good, called Digress; let's try that.

Croatia: Okay.

At this point, the Italian girl is cold, and doesn't make eye contact. Her Croatian friend sees we are friendly people and is probably thinking free drinks!

Richard: This way! [*as Italian girl goes the wrong way*]

We lead them across the road. We slightly separate at the bar to let the girls buy their own drinks (I might buy a girl a drink, but never this soon, and never her friends too). We chat, come back to them. I talk to the Croatian girl (Dubravka) because I wanted my friend to try his luck with Eva. I connect well with Dubravka, exchange some light banter, but try not to generate too much attraction since I'm not interested in her. My friend isn't progressing things with the Italian girl, and goes to the bar. I engage them both and then switch to Eva when he comes back, leaving him to wing her friend. I ask some boring questions but connect well.

Richard: Do you like London?

Eva: Yes, I love London.

Richard: London's a great city, it has a pretty unique feel; it's very mixed culturally and even has a mix of historical and modern . . . What's your profession?

Eva: I'm a scientist.

Richard: Wow, a sexy scientist, that's cool. [*smiles*] What's your area?

Eva: Cancer.

Richard: You must be very passionate about helping people and making a difference. I like that – most people work just for money, it's nice to meet someone who does something for the good of mankind. That is why you do it, right?

Eva: Yes, I love what I do. I couldn't do anything else. What do you do?

Richard: I'm a life coach.

Eva: So you help people too?

Richard: Yeah, I guess so; I wouldn't like to say it is as important, or that I do it just because I'm a good person. [*I sense some connection so want to dial it up a bit.*] What compliment do guys normally give you?

Eva: Usually about my eyes.

Richard: Your eyes are nice, but mainly because you always seem to be smiling with your eyes. I love your hair! What actress do people say you look like?

Eva: Monica Bellucci.

Richard: Hmmm, I don't know, maybe, but to me, you look more like Sandra Bullock or Eva Longoria. Who do I look like?

Eva: You look like Ethan Hawke.

Richard: Ethan Hawke? Do you like Ethan Hawke [*with smirk*]?

Eva: Yes

Richard: I like Sandra Bullock [*seductive face*].

First verbal one-on-one: I decide at this point to bring them along to the club we were planning to go to. I call the club and add the two girls to the guest list. The attraction is there, there is some sexual tension. I find that when I create tension the girl will enjoy the wait for the kiss, rather than wondering, "When is this idiot going to kiss me?"

On the way to the club, my friend is bantering; we make some jokes, he teases Dubravka. This mixes up the mood a bit, which is good. We give a little demonstration of value by breezing in to the club for free without queuing. I ask if they'd like to share a bottle of wine. They say yes, we buy it and collect half the money from them.

Crystal is a club where, in order to sit down, you need to get a table, and to get a table you need to spend hundreds or thousands on bottles of champagne or vodka. I managed to work the staff and get us on a table for twelve. We were the only ones with a £20 bottle of wine, everyone else at the tables was a big spender.

We take our seat and, unfortunately, I make a little mistake because I don't pay attention, and she sits adjacent to me instead of next to me. I'm still close enough to touch, but it's not as intimate as I'd like. I decide to leave things as they are instead of asking people to move around. I also work to nullify any future objections:

Richard: I'm glad we met in the street and not in a club. I don't like to meet girls in bars. It was amazing how we met, because, if either of us left the bar just ten seconds earlier or later, we never would have seen each other. We could go back further about the decision to go to that particular place, or even further, about how our parents met [*connecting and deepening the connection, suggesting fate*]. When are you going back?

Eva: In two days.

Richard: Well, we better not fall in love tonight then [*gazes into her eyes*]. How many times have you been in love?

Eva: Twice. You?

Richard: Definitely once, maybe twice. You seem like an independent woman, so you probably want a man that also has clear goals and a vision so that together you can be *more*. I think because you're independent you don't feel a desperate need to find a man, but you would like the right one. A relationship where together you're worth more than apart. I don't think you'd like to be tied down or to just be lazy. I think you've so many things that you want to do and barely enough time to do them. [*She is nodding away, very attracted.*] Are your friends mostly men or women?

Eva: Men. I get on better with men.

Richard: My friends are mostly women, male friends can get jealous and it's rare to find one who would be truly happy for me if really good things happened. There is always some competitiveness. My female friends would all be happy for me if something good happened.

Eva: What kind of girl do you like?

Richard: I look for a girl who has her life together, who is content with what she has, that doesn't *need* a man, but wants one who will make her happier. A relationship where together we equal more than if we're apart. Do you smoke?

Eva: No.

Richard: Good. What colour are your eyes?

Eva: Brown. [*We get close and look into each other's eyes.*] Yours are green. [*I stop talking, smile, look at her lips.*]

Richard: If you were in kissing school, what grade would you get?

Eva: Definitely an 'A'.

Richard: An 'A'? No way! Only a small percentage can get an 'A'.

She knows I know I can kiss her, but I lean in a bit, then come back out and make her wait a bit more. I'm trying out a new thing, building up loads of sexual tension. Also I liked this girl, so I don't want to use the cheesy kissing school close.

Eva: How old are you?

Richard: Twenty-six, I don't normally date girls over twenty-four! You tricked me, you look young, you must have good moisturiser [*strokes face with back of index finger*].

Notice I'm in a qualifying phase, where I keep challenging her in a way that shows I have high standards and certain requirements that need to be met.

Richard: You're a good girl, but I think you know how to have fun!

Eva: Yes I do.

Richard: [*I lean in as I speak and get the kiss.*] Hmmm, nice, B+ with room for improvement. Can you dance?

Eva: Yes.

I take her to dance by the table; the dancing gets sexy, then I lead her to dance on the back of the seats in the middle of the club. We stand out and it's pretty crazy, it gets us lots of attention. I'm kissing her, grinding, and when the song 'Smack That' comes on I'm smacking her ass. It escalates a lot. The club is too noisy now to talk; I kiss her neck, touch the back of her hair, I'm going for sensual over sexual.

Richard: How tall are you?

Eva: One hundred and seventy-three centimetres [*look of semi-approval*].

The other two look a bit tired and bored; it's getting late so I suggest we leave. We come out of the club and it turns out that their bus home goes from very near my house, so I make like we are leading them to the bus. When we are right near my house, I say:

Richard: Let's go for a drink somewhere else.

Eva: Okay, where?

Richard: I live just there, I have some nice wine. [*I would normally have to work harder but think that in this case it was on already.*]

My friend tells the other girl we are going to 'Club Rich'. We take them to the house. Inside, we sit in the kitchen; I give her some time to relax and get comfortable, then I say I'll put some music on and tell her, "Come and choose." She comes to my room, we put the music on, I close the door. I like this girl a lot, so I'm happy to take my time and escalate pretty slowly, keeping the tension there and letting her know that I'm in control. We have sex. Her friend is still in the kitchen and is pretty pissed off. Our friends don't really want each other that much, even though they kissed in the club. I say it's a shame she can't stay; we could talk more and have a nice breakfast.

Richard: I wish I had another hour to talk to you, there's lots more we need to know about each other.

We walk them to their bus and say goodbye.

She leaves in two days; I don't see her again in London because she needs to make it up to her poor best friend. I get a text when she gets back home to Italy, asking me to come and visit. I'm planning to go when disaster strikes. I get a text that reads, "I could have fallen for the boy that wanted to be a teacher, but not Gambler, someone who seduces women for an experiment."

I was with a friend when I read this and I was crushed; he thought it was pretty funny. I felt sick; we had made the most fantastic connection and it had been ruined. I felt like crying. She'd googled me and found the PUAtraining.com website. The way I'm presented on this website is not really how I am. For marketing reasons, it needs to be sold like 'Get Laid Today!' In reality, what I teach is pretty wholesome; ex-girlfriends work for me on the event, we have a female trainer. I love women and never mistreat them, or try to trick them into bed.

I went home and called her; she answered. I spent about forty minutes trying to tell her that the emotion we had was genuine, that she can think about it and see that I didn't use any tricks or gimmicks on her, that it was natural and spontaneous.

Over the next few days I gradually turn her around. She wants to believe that it was real, and it was; my impression on the night was so strong that she still wants to see me, and says she loves me. I book my flight a couple of days after the initial text message. I visit her in Milan, we have a pretty good time, but it just isn't as good as it was in

London. She has a fantastic body, a pretty face, she's intelligent, but I think there is one thing missing. She lacked passion, and was a bit unemotional or repressed. It's important to me that the girl expresses her emotions and passions in the way she looks at me, the way she speaks, what she says, and, of course, in bed.

We have a good weekend and plan to meet again in the future, but it is obviously not something that is going to the next level.

KISS CLOSING

This is a sticking point for lots of guys. Going for the kiss is another point where you're putting yourself in a position to get rejected. The way to remove the pressure from this moment is to work up to it smoothly with a variety of escalation techniques, and by using tests to see if the girl is ready. If you're not in the seductive character at the time of the kiss, she might not feel in the mood! Here are the techniques to make the kiss a smooth move she'll go for every time:

1. Touch her in increasingly more sensual ways leading up to the kiss:

- Touch her arm for emphasis when you're talking.
- Touch her hand. Looking at jewellery is a good excuse.
- Touch her hair. Asking if it's her natural colour/if she ever wears it up/has ever cut it short/used to have it long/or even when she washed it is a good excuse. If

she is comfortable with you touching her hair and doesn't recoil at all, then she is kissable. You can go for it here.

• Smell her hair.

• Take her hand and hold it as you talk. If you've done the above, it will be acceptable at this point. Don't look at her hand or draw attention to it, just do it.

• Squeeze her hand and see if she squeezes back; this is another kissability indicator. No girl ever squeezes back if she isn't ready to kiss.

• Stop talking, pause, tilt your head and look at her. See if she is comfortable. If she is, you can kiss.

• What if she turns her face when you try to kiss? Kiss her cheek and then her neck! She'll turn around and kiss you. This is not a rejection, but most guys assume it to be and back away. Do this and you can turn her on even more. It's only a rejection if she recoils – backs off and away.

So now you know how to touch her, but it will still not be a hundred per cent smooth if you're still in the same character as when talking to your hairdresser – i.e. acting like a friend instead of a lover. Remember 'The Three Characters of a Seduction'? It's time for the Seducer . . .

2. Establish a sexual vibe as you escalate the physical contact. You do this by:

   • More intense eye contact

- Slower, smoother, deeper voice.
- Look at her in a sexual way, start to look at her lips as well as her eyes and see if she reciprocates. If she does, she is imagining kissing you.

3. Sometimes, even with no work on your part, she'll want you. When a girl wants to kiss you:
  - She squeezes your hand.
  - She looks at your lips.
  - She touches your chest instead of your arm.
  - She is comfortable with hard eye contact even when no one is speaking.

SAME-NIGHT SEX

I believe that every girl is persuadable! I'm not going to use the term 'one-night stand', but I will say 'same-night sex'. This means sleeping with the girl the night you meet her, but you may well see her again. I always try to sleep with the girl as quickly as possible, even if I'm aiming for a relationship, because it just makes things so much easier once it's out of the way.

Why go for same-night sex?

Sometimes you meet and feel a huge sexual vibe. If you took her number to meet another time, it might be gone. I'm able to get a very strong connection with a girl very quickly from my conversations; I can generate attraction on a lot of levels. Anyway, I've had my best experiences when things seem just perfect on the same night I meet a girl. If you want a casual relationship, sleeping with them before they know you well enough to become emotionally attached is the right policy. If you want something deeper, sleeping with them quickly so that you can both become more relaxed with each other is also the right policy.

Remember, I'm a pick-up artist, I'm not grabbing ugly, drunk girls off the dance-floor at 2am. I'm meeting a beautiful girl, usually the best in the club, at 10pm and getting to know her, then taking her home later (usually!). This means we can create a romantic, intimate, passionate experience. I love romance, those Hollywood moments; I don't like sex in the bathroom. And I think you can get this on the same night if you're both pretty sober and have more than a physical connection. I've done everything from twenty minutes street-to-house with a super-hot model (the hottest girl I ever slept with) to a ten-hour marathon of objections from a virgin. (I wasn't being a bastard, she became my GF!) There are different types of same-night sex and it generally depends on the girl.

Easy

You have girls that have lots of one-night stands and are open to it, they want it. What appeals to them is a dominant man who looks like he can take care of them sexually. He should make all the outward displays of confidence, approach directly and escalate smoothly from touching to kissing to grinding, telling her what he wants to do with her, etc. With this girl, you can simply lead her out of the club and there won't be any questions asked about what is going on. "Where's your jacket? Let's get out of here!"

Medium

There are other girls that have maybe tried it once, but it isn't something they look for. They are not sluts and don't want to be considered as such, but they still enjoy sex and aren't prudish. These girls need more than the physical, and will reject you if that is all that's on offer. You can give them a taste, but should also be slowing down to show you have self-control and to take the time to get to know each other.

She needs to feel that Hollywood moment, like she has met a fantastic guy. It's then okay to do it with you, because you're special and tonight is special. Stare into her eyes in a loving way, find out stuff about her and connect on it. Then show how you become more and more attracted to her as you find out more about her. You need to connect on emotions, to show your emotional side as a modern man. However, underneath there is sexual tension in the way you look at her. In summary, turn her on mentally, emotionally and physically.

You'll need a reason for this girl to come home with you – hearing you play a song, seeing some pictures or your cute dog. You should tell her, "Let's go somewhere else," and then, when she asks where, you can say, "I want to show you something," and just take her to your place. You'll meet objections on the way if she finds out where you are taking her. You can say, "Well, you can't stay long, I need to wake up early," and then quickly change the subject. DO NOT ENGAGE IN LOGICAL DEBATE. Keep leading her and change the subject.

If she objects to you verbally but still consents physically (i.e. she says she shouldn't go back with you but is still walking hand in hand), it's a token objection and can be quickly dealt with. If she objects to you physically and verbally, stop what you're doing, she is not going to come home with you or do anything with you. Respect her and stop it there! Learn this important point. Women sometimes like to object and wrestle with you, if they want to be controlled. This can make it difficult for the man because of the very real problem of rape. By following this simple rule, you will be sure that you are respecting her.

If she only objects to you physically but looks like she is enjoying it, wants you to hold her down and isn't making any verbal complaint, she is just turning herself on. You can continue. But make sure you judge it right! If you're hurting her rather than just controlling her physically, in my opinion that's also going too far – even if she likes it!

Advanced

The third type of girl is the one that's not very sexual and will always react in horror at the thought of a 'dirty' one-night stand, or sleeping with a guy so quickly. Connect with her on an emotional level. Have a tiny bit of sexual tension, just enough to generate attraction and avoid being thought of as a friend.

Getting her back to the house won't be too difficult, because you'll generate trust and you *won't kiss her* before you get there. You connect on all levels, then make the excuse to go somewhere more quiet, more comfortable, where the drinks are cheaper, to chat some more. You need to talk about future plans with this girl, things you can do together. If there are any objections, you should manage to get around them with, "I want to show you where I live. Anyway . . ." Get to the house. Sit her on your bed. Get the wine out. Give her time to get comfortable. After five minutes, go in for the kiss. Remember that you could have kissed earlier because you have comfort, trust, connection and attraction, but you waited to avoid the "Oh, I'm horny now, let's go to my place" vibe. The kiss has been 'on' for a while so it's easy.

You kiss, you brush your hand over her breast. You escalate very slowly and smoothly. You undo her bra before taking her top off. You touch her boobs. You touch her pussy via the back of her pants before taking them off. You put her hand on your penis because she won't do it herself. Any time you sense discomfort on her part, take a

174

step back, keep it there and then re-escalate. Have an excuse to get in the bed (it's more comfortable); have an excuse to take clothes off (it's hot), all while physically escalating. It's got to be like it happened by accident. Once she is naked, it has passed the point of no return and should be plain sailing.

Girls will be much more likely to go home with you if you do not directly imply they're coming back to have sex with you. Of course, they will know it on some level, but a much higher percentage of girls will sleep with you just from the subtle substitution of "Want to go back and have sex with me?" with "Want to come for coffee?", which makes it slightly more likely. "Want to go someplace more comfortable?" and "Let's go somewhere else" make it more likely still.

The difference is that you're leading, not asking. People feel more comfortable in simply following rather than making a commitment to follow. For example, "Let's go dance" always works better than "Would you like to dance?"

Tips
Dirty dancing is generally good for getting in the mood, getting her comfortable with you physically, etc. You need to be confident and comfortable so that she feels that vibe, too. Treat her like your girlfriend. Touch her with familiarity. Awkwardness won't fly.

Logistics

Is she able to leave her friends, is she driving them home or does she have other commitments? Is your place/her place close by? (It helps a lot if it is.)

EVOLUTION OF A NATURAL: FEBRUARY 2007

By this time, I really felt like I had reached another level. Months before, I'd been able to meet girls and get dates, but I had been uncomfortable in classy venues and hadn't had a truly stunning girl. In December I'd slept with a girl whose looks were one in a hundred thousand, and in January I'd dated a girl who was similarly blessed intellectually. I was, however, surrounded by some other guys – especially those who worked with me at PUATraining, who slept with multiple girls week in, week out. I'd never had sex with a girl just for the sake of having sex. My sex drive isn't so high that I need lots of women. If I have sex with a girl, I usually want there to be some connection other than the physical, so a one-night stand does little for me. Learning to be good at picking up women is more about being able to attract a higher standard of girlfriend, rather than having a huge number of notches on the bedpost.

I think that we are all influenced by our peers, however, and I did wonder at times whether I should be having sex with loads of different girls.

One night in Tiger Tiger, I saw a girl that was attractive but not amazingly so, and I happened to approach pretty directly. I saw her; she looked at me; I went straight up and sat next to her, putting my arm around her. She was Swedish, worked in a women's underwear shop, and was dressed very sexily in a corset. I asked her name and chatted about boring stuff, but I was doing it in a seductive way. I was touching the back of her head and neck and her hair. I pulled her hair lightly and she said, "You better pull my hair tonight." That was the most direct thing I'd heard from a girl after such a short amount of time. Her friends were there, and they interrupted for a while. Then she asked me where I lived. I told her and she said, "Good, it's not far for me to walk to work in the morning." I just said, "Let's go," and within twenty minutes of meeting her we were walking to my house. I'd taken girls back before, but it'd never been so obvious what was going to happen.

We got back to my room and had sex. I'd done something I'd not really done before, which was a real one-night stand; I'd slept with girls on the first date, and on the first night I'd met them, but there was always more of a connection and they were never so direct about it. She left in the morning, didn't leave her number, didn't ask for mine. I'm glad I tried this, but it really didn't leave me feeling fulfilled. I decided that I probably wouldn't have many more one-night stands. I would sleep with girls sooner, but I didn't want to get in the habit of barely knowing who I slept with.

This month I had another first: my first English

girlfriend! I'd kissed English girls, but I'd never had an English girlfriend. Generally, I prefer the looks of Scandinavian, Russian or South American girls, and I prefer their characters too. London does have lots of foreign girls, but I wasn't purposefully avoiding English girls – I'd just see someone I fancied and they'd turn out to be from another country, or at least have some mixed heritage.

Karen was another Tiger Tiger girl. I was there on the Saturday night of our weekend training event, standing with some students. There were four girls over my shoulder. They were taking pictures of each other, so I went in and gave them a lesson on how to pose. They took more pictures and I integrated into the group. I brought in the students for the other girls and then concentrated on Karen, who was the most attractive. She was tall, slim, a natural blonde with blue eyes, definitely an attractive girl. I moved around her so that she faced me and not her friends, and so had 'pseudo-isolation' – with her friends, but not with them.

We talked and I quickly started challenging: "Do you smoke?" She saw my face and calculated her response. "Sometimes, but I'm trying to quit!" After that she was chasing me, re-initiating the conversation and giving compliments. Sexual tension was building quickly through the eye contact, and after five to ten minutes I noticed that she had cocked her head to one side. This was a big indicator of sexual interest, and I moved in for the kiss. We kissed, and danced. But I was working as a trainer that night

178

and, although it is good to demo and help out the guys by winging, if I stay in a set for hours it's not so great for the students. For this reason I took her number and made my excuses to leave.

I called her a few days later and got the "Hi! How are you?" kind of answer that shows she was really looking forward to my call. Our first date was dinner at her house! I went round and she cooked for me. It was nice; we fooled around on her bed while watching a film; she asked if I wanted to stay, but I got the last train home. She had some resistance about having sex on the first date, so I didn't push it because I knew I would see her again. The conversation was pretty good, and I think I liked her because she was different to all the other girls I'd dated.

We talked a lot on the phone and arranged a second date. I had it all planned out, I'd meet her and take her to the games arcade. This sounds stupid, but a few times previously I'd taken girls there and we played the physical games – dancing, playing the drums, etc., and it was really fun. But she was a bit less adventurous, and felt like a fish out of water. That was fine, we didn't stay long and went for dinner. I wanted to take her to the Salsa bar, where we could eat and watch people dancing and maybe dance a bit ourselves. I'd been there with a client for dinner and it was really cool. Unfortunately, this time it was a Saturday night and so super noisy that we couldn't even hear each other talking across the table. So I was zero out of two so far.

We went back to my house and cooked pancakes for

dessert, because it was close to pancake day. I almost never get ill, but I had the sniffles that night and kept needing to blow my nose. It was all blocked up and I couldn't taste my food properly. We ate our pancakes, and then I took her into my room and started kissing her. We lay down on the bed and things escalated. I was kissing her, but my nose kept running! I had to stop, say sorry, and go get tissues. I think that, while I was kissing her, my wet nose left its trail on her face. I didn't feel good at all, but we kept on going. I also needed to go to the toilet but didn't want to break the action. We undressed, got in the bed and started to have sex. I lasted about five minutes! I think it was a combination of needing to go to the toilet and being ill, but it was my worst performance ever. I took her back to the train station and saw her off. She didn't call me again, and I didn't call her. Partly it was embarrassment, and partly realisation that we weren't right for each other. People ask me how I break up with girls without hurting them. This was not pre-planned, but a date like this would probably work to put a girl off in most cases! She was an investment banker, and going out with her was a novelty I enjoyed for a few hours. But there was no connection there, and this relationship reinforced my preference for foreign girls.

SEX ON A FIRST DATE

Most guys meet girls for dates after a number close and see the attraction completely fizzle out; or, at a minimum, they take a number of dates to get into a position where they can take things physical. Meeting her for lunch or in a coffee shop in the daytime are mistakes. There is a way to close eighty per cent-plus of girls on a first date, even from a five-minute number close.

You need a set pattern to these dates. It's in your interest to sleep with a girl quickly. Whether you only want something casual with her, or you want her for your girlfriend, either way you should sleep with her quickly. If you want a casual relationship, you'll achieve your goal quickly; if you want a girlfriend, it makes things a whole lot less complicated. So how do you do it? There are a few essential elements. Meet at night. There is more of a sexual vibe at night, so you can establish it straight away. Meet somewhere near where you live, preferably within walking distance. I arrange this with a girl by saying, "Let's meet in Covent Garden; when's good for you, 8 or 9pm?" The question offers illusory choice on a point that's irrelevant to me in terms of the result.

When you meet her, the most important thing to do is immediately treat her as if she's your girlfriend. Kiss her on the cheek, take her hand or put your arm around her, and lead her off to the location of your date. Remember that, if she meets you for a date, she is attracted to you. By treating her as your girlfriend, you're basically triggering all the feelings within her associated with guys she has dated for years. You're touching her like her ex-boyfriends. You're comfortable and she'll be comfortable. When you're uncomfortable and nervous, she'll be the same.

181

When you arrive at your destination, let her sit first and then sit next to her. You'll be in danger of losing the sexual vibe if you sit opposite her. In terms of conversation, mix playfulness, teasing, the sexual vibe and comfort-building. For my date, I take her to a spot that closes at 11pm, so it's natural to leave and then just lead her to my house. If you don't have a place like that, you can say, "Let's go somewhere else," and lead her. When you're walking down the road, don't talk about where you're going. If she asks directly, you can say, "We are going somewhere more comfortable where the drinks are cheaper," or even "I'm going to show you where I live." You can also have an excuse to take her home, like "Come and see my cat do back-flips".

The key thing here is to immediately distract her; ask or talk about something else. "So, did you watch that new film?" Then continue leading her and walking. If she objects to you verbally but is still walking with you, do not engage in logical debate. Remember that a woman has both a logical and an emotional mind. Her emotional mind is expressed through her body and her logical mind through her speech. Distract her logical mind.

When you get back to the house, sit her down (on your bed if possible!) and give her some space. Do not get in her face straight away. You're doing some crucial things here, like showing that you have self-control. This generates trust, and she'll feel more comfortable with you.

After a few minutes, go into the seductive character

again and build some tension before you kiss her; that will make the kiss more passionate and will turn her on. Kiss for a bit, then lay her down. If she isn't in your bedroom, give her the tour; have something in your room that you can look at together, and do it sitting on the bed. Slowly escalate. Kiss her neck and nibble her ear. Touch her boobs first by stroking your hand from her shoulder down to her waist, touching them incidentally. Undo her bra without taking her top off. Touch her boobs under her shirt, then take both your tops off. Touch her ass down the back of her trousers and her pussy in the same way. When she is hot and horny, unbutton her trousers and get them off. From there it should be plain sailing.

If you get an objection or sense one coming, go back a step and turn her on some more – then go for it smoothly again.

EVOLUTION OF A NATURAL: MARCH 2007

I had a lot of great nights in March. I'd been getting some pretty cool party invites, but hadn't really capitalised on them that much in terms of meeting very hot girls. Initially I wanted to attend these events to pitch the business to rich but unsatisfied men, but I have trouble networking because I don't like selling to people and I don't like acting fake. If I meet someone who I like and who can offer me something, that's fine, but I don't like trying to make friends with someone just because I think they can offer

183

me something. So one night in March, I got an invite to a bar in South Kensington called Collection. It was a fashion party, and when we turned up they had free drinks.

I should state here that I do drink sometimes. I didn't drink for many months, but when I go to a party with free drinks I usually have a few. It is very important not to use alcohol (or drugs!) as a crutch, something you *need* in order to talk to women, but that doesn't mean you can't drink occasionally.

On this occasion, I drank! They had free champagne and cocktails, and I got tipsy. I was with Anthony and Steve, my good friends, and we were hanging around even though there were plenty of hot girls, including models from the fashion show. A massage girl asked me if I wanted a massage; I didn't, but we got talking and she said she'd give me a free one later. Steve said, "Why are you talking to her when all these models are here?" and it got on my nerves because he hadn't talked to anyone. I kind of wanted to show him what's what, and, when Anthony pointed out a very hot girl five metres away, Steve's expression showed he thought she was stunning. She was taking pictures of the show, and I got her attention by posing for her in a funny, model-ish way; she laughed. I decided to go and talk to her, but she was in a very difficult-to-get-to position, I couldn't just casually wander over. I had to get through a bunch of people, walk through a restaurant and ask some others to move out of the way; when I got there she was with her friend, which made things even more difficult. I opened by asking to see the pics she took of me, we had a nice chat, I flirted and took her number (first number close). She was stunning, a model, intelligent. I planned to chat to her some more later.

At this moment, the massage girl came over and offered me the free massage. It was very nice (best part – the ears!), and she was talking to me the whole time, obviously very interested. Whilst she was working away I was checking out a hot model in front of me, who looked Russian and rather cat-like. After she finished, the massage girl went off to find some paying customers; I went up behind the Russian model and started massaging her. She liked it, she turned around, we chatted; I told her she looked like a cat, which hooked her since she had cats and loved them. I also guessed correctly that she was Russian, as well as a model! She was one in twenty thousand in terms of looks, simply stunning. She had a boyfriend, but didn't seem to be very into him, and I got her number (second number close). I moved to the other end of the bar and chatted to a hot Australian girl; after a few minutes I found out she had a boyfriend (who she was obviously into), and she introduced me to her friend from Croatia; she was nice, another model, I got her number in one minute (third number close). I walked back to the middle of the bar, was going to talk to my friends but got chatting to the massage girl again. They were not allowed to give their numbers, so I set my phone to record and pretended I was on a call whilst taking it (fourth number close). I liked this one, and had some great conversations with her over the course of the evening.

I go back to my friends, and am so in state that I just ask Anthony P to point out the next one for me to go to. He says the waitress is cute so I go right in there. Conversation is good, she laughs, she is attracted to me but can't give her number, so I use the recording trick again (fifth number close). I've got the number of all the hot girls in the bar, including two that would be fired for giving it to me and three models. Have another chat with the first girl, kiss her, she is going home with her friends so I can't take it any further. I get my coat and number-close the coat-check girl for good measure (sixth number close). The best thing about this night wasn't that I got six numbers, it was that four of the girls whose numbers I got were very beautiful, very high value, every guy in the place wanted them, but I was the only one to get any of them. And I got *all* of them. I'd got this many before in a night, but normally I'd only get a number from a girl of this quality once every month!

This was later dubbed 'the night of the high winds', and was talked about for weeks. Steve said he'd never seen anything like it and didn't know anyone on earth who could do what I'd just done. The high from that night lasted for weeks, and any time I doubt myself I can look back at what happened! In fact, the vibe definitely lasted a couple more nights, because two days later we went to . . .

Stringfellows

I sat with Anthony at a table with our beers, having used our free entry pass to get in. We never pay to get in the strip club, won't have more than one drink, and never pay for dances. If we like the girl, we want to see her outside the club, and if we don't like her we don't want to pay for a dance.

A girl is talking to Anthony, whilst another comes to sit at the table. She doesn't talk to me and I ignore her for a while. She looks like a high priestess from an old film, wearing a white flowing dress, unlike what the other girls wear, and with a flower in her hair. After a few minutes I break the silence. She is drinking water with tons of lemon in it, says it's for her health. We chat; she is half-Greek, half-Brazilian, called Carol. I find out she has been in London for a few months, but doesn't have any friends and wants to go out and dance in a proper club. I tell her that I go to lots of clubs. I can tell she is interested when she asks why I'm there, because I'm not like the other guys. I say we need to meet up. She says she doesn't know her number, which is usually a blow-off, but I can tell that it's true in this case. She tells me to write my number down. I go to the bathroom, borrow a pen from the toilet guy, write my number on a travelcard and go and give it to her. She puts it in her shoe and gets on with dancing. She calls me a day or two later and says she has been trying lots of numbers because she couldn't read what I wrote (something to do with the English vs. European way of writing a seven); I take her perseverance as a very positive sign and suggest we meet the next night at a bar. I'm planning to have a quick drink and then get her back to my house. I think it's a bold move which could work, but she surprises me. She says, "No, baby, you will buy some wine and I will come to your house!" Excellent! Come the evening, I meet her at the local tube station and walk her back to my house. We sit on the sofa and I pour the wine. We small-talk, and, after a few sips, all it takes is one sexual look from me and she gets on top and starts kissing me. She is happy to take the initiative, she takes her clothes off (but I guess she is used to doing that) and I pick her up and take her to bed. Things move swiftly, but she tells me that she has her period that day. We carry on kissing, and she rubs herself on my leg with her knickers on. Then she says, "Would you like to fuck me in the ass?" I say, "Okay." I'd never done it before, but that's exactly what I do. She takes my hand and makes me slap her ass too. She has no worries about showing me what she likes. It's a pretty memorable experience, and the best thing for me was that I was finally able to handle myself with a *very* sexually confident girl.

Later she tells me that she has slept with tons of guys, a few girls, and had some crazy sexual experiences.

She comes around more times over the next month. I

don't like the expression 'fuck buddies', but if ever there was a relationship of mine that could be classified like that it was this one. We *did* go to eat together, and watch a film, and we like each other on some level – but we are not compatible, and we both know there is no long-term relationship there.

I thought that the first experience with her was as wild as it could get, but there was more to come! On our second 'date', she put on one of my ties, got me to take sexy pics of her, and to choke her, pull her hair and slap her ass almost simultaneously as we had sex. I didn't go the whole way and start calling her a bitch, like she wanted me to, but this was something pretty far removed from what I was used to.

She told me she liked the way I mixed tenderness and roughness. Basically what she wanted was a man who would stroke her face, then slap it. Pretty crazy. It wasn't exactly my style, but I must say it changed me somewhat. I really appreciated her sexually aggressive ways, and her skills – she knew exactly how to turn a man on. Usually I'd have sex twice at the most in one night, but with this girl she'd be able to turn me back on *every single time*. Usually girls try things that men don't really like, they try their best but don't really know what a man wants. She knew *exactly* what to do!

Almost like the introvert that adds in the extrovert skills, I'd added a dirtier side to my sexual skills to complement the tender side that existed already. The biggest ego-boost of this whole experience was when she said I was very good, and that came from a girl who had slept with many guys and knew exactly what she wanted.

Boot-camp demo

A few days later, I was doing a weekend boot-camp, training the guys on a Saturday night in a West End nightclub. I met a girl on the stairs, talked with her for a bit and then brought her downstairs to meet my friends. I sat down with her and all the boot-camp students were around. It was quiet in the restaurant area of the club, so they could all see and hear what I was doing. I introduced her and then chatted directly to her. I was talking about normal stuff, but at the same time I was running my hand up her back, touching her neck and the back of her head, and she was loving it. I told Rich, a trainer on the boot-camps, that I was going to kiss her within one minute; he told the rest of the boys and they were all watching. It must have been pretty funny.

We are talking about whether she has ever kissed a girl, and she says she's slightly bisexual. I tell her a story in an increasingly seductive voice that Carol told me a few days ago, about when she'd been on an island in Greece and fancied a girl who had a boyfriend. "They'd exchange glances and she felt some sexual tension, but the guy was always there. Then one day, she was lying in a jacuzzi with her eyes closed and her head resting on the side, basking in the sun, when she noticed the sun getting blocked out by something and then felt soft hair on her face, and then someone getting very close [I do this to her at the same time] and slowly working her way across to her lips, and then she felt a gentle kiss that made her shiver." At this point I kiss her and it is very, very sexy. She wants to sleep with me, and I do find her attractive, but I'm very tired from the boot-camp and I send her back to her friends. The guys love it; they love how she was so attracted to me, they love the way I could do it even with them there, almost on call.

Day Game

DAY GAME AND NIGHT GAME ARE DIFFERENT, AND YOU'LL PROBABLY PREFER ONE OR THE OTHER. There are benefits and drawbacks to each. Day game means game outside of bars and clubs. It covers street game, shops, gym, public transport, etc., and has a lot of benefits and differences compared to night game. Day game allows you to approach girls who are on their own (they probably won't be at night!) and not used to getting hit on in these situations, so they don't have bitch-shields.

You'll be getting the real person: most people have a persona that they adopt in a club. Because you're both sober and being yourselves, any number you get in the daytime is a lot more solid. Girls often flake on club number closes because they were drunk and don't like the idea of meeting a guy in a bar. Daytime approaches are the opposite; they are actually romantic, and telling her friends she is meeting "the guy that chatted me up in the post office" is much better than "the guy I met in a bar on Friday night". There are also lots of attractive girls who avoid going out at night because they don't like nasty men groping them, don't like loud music or just prefer to do other things. If you want to meet a nice girlfriend who won't cheat on you, and isn't a party girl who likes getting drunk, day game is the way to go.

The problem with day game is that the girls you approach will be more difficult to hook. Girls in the daytime are doing something; they are on their way somewhere, waiting for someone, buying something or doing their workout. You can open any group standing around in a bar, and holding them for a minute shouldn't be too much of a problem. A girl walking in the street will only stop for you if you've a very good reason to stop her (asking if you should dye your hair generally won't cut it!), and it will take a lot for you to distract her from whatever she's doing.

Day game is a more advanced skill because it works best when you can use something spontaneous and situational to start the conversation. Canned material, opinion openers, routines and magic tricks just seem a little weird in the day. Day game is really more about your natural conversational skills and personality, and one drawback is that it's difficult to kino-escalate. A one-minute kiss close in the daytime is an advanced-level skill.

Optional and Advanced Techniques

WINGING

WINGING IS WHEN YOU'RE WORKING TOGETHER WITH A FRIEND TO MEET MORE GIRLS. It can greatly increase your chances. If you're alone you can approach lone girls, and you can approach groups to try to isolate your target girl. But it can sometimes be tricky, especially when starting out. If you have a wing, when you approach a pair of girls you can isolate almost immediately, and don't need the ability to hold a large group for a long time. Together you should achieve more. Sometimes one of you will have to talk to girls you're not attracted to, but it all balances out. There are various ways to wing together, some of the best approaches are:

You stand near the girls, have fun together and react to what each other says, then open the girls seemingly spontaneously: "[*to friend*] No way! Hey, guys, do I look gay? He just said I look gay in this shirt!"

One of you approaches and opens the whole group; the other friend wanders in once the group is hooked. If it's a pair of girls, you can both isolate. With a bigger group, one guy should take out the rest while one has the target isolated. This could be the guy who opened or the one who comes in.

With a mixed group, I find it's best to open the guys first and make friends with them. While this is going on, the wing comes in and takes the target. The guy that opens the group is doing the harder work — he should have first choice over which girl he wants!

Other things that wings can do include:
Accomplishment intros: "This is my friend, he has the coolest job — he lives at the bottom of the sea!" What you're doing is making your friend sound cool in some way. If he did it himself, it would be bragging, but if you do it it's fine.

Where's Michelle?: A pick-up artist called Toecutter came up with this one. The wing will come into the group and ask if you've seen Michelle. You say you think she is over there. He turns to leave; if you want him in the interaction, you pull him back in and introduce him. If not, you let him go.

Code words: You can work out code words with your wing: for example, for location changing ("I like this song"), taking the girls home ("want some gum?"), identifying your target ("this one is trouble"), etc.

The importance of having fun with your wings in a non-club environment:

Do competitive fun activities – sports, games, the arcade, bowling. Harness upbeat high-energy. If your only connection is skulking around looking for chicks, it won't be as interesting. Find some stories to tell, have loads of fun and then bring the party to the location.

AMOGING AND DISARMING – DEALING WITH OTHER GUYS

AMOGing is the process of putting another male in a lower position than you. (AMOG stands for Alpha Male Of Group.) You assert your 'alpha-ness' over the other man to make yourself look better. Obviously, the leader of men is more attractive to women, so this increases your chances of picking up. You need to have higher status than the other males. I don't endorse these tactics, but it's good to be aware of them so that you can see when guys try them on you:

- Backslapping and putting your arm around him are two ways to physically AMOG a guy.
- The alpha handshake – when you shake hands, come in high with your hand pointing downwards, shake his hand and turn to put it in the lower position, palm up. As an added insult, take their elbow as you shake and then slap them on the back afterwards.
- Use Tyler Durden's "Hey, that's a great shirt – look at

those cool stripes, my mum bought me one of those in high school," and similar variations.

- Don't answer a question he asks you.
- Ignore him and carry on talking to the girls if he tries to say something.
- Get between him and the girl(s) and turn your back to him.
- He might ask you a question about your job, your clothes, whether you work out, or something else with the goal of saying, "I'm richer than you," or "I'm tougher than you." If he does this, you should say, "Oooh no, it's really cheap," or "Oh, you're much stronger than me." He won't know what to say and will look stupid.
- If the guy talks about how great he is, agree and say something like, "Wow, you must be really proud of yourself!"
- If he looks really cool and alpha, say, "Girls, look how cool this guy is – look at how he stands with his legs wide apart and has that cool James Bond look on his face." He'll become self-conscious and lose the plot.

Disarming

Disarming is the process of befriending a male in a group, or otherwise taking away the threat of him ruining the interaction for you. It is a much better tactic than AMOG. To disarm, you can open the guy first, pay him lots of compliments and make him feel good, then ask how he knows the girls, get introduced and work your way round to them. Guys rarely get compliments, so it's pretty easy to do this and make them like you. Gaming guys is easier than gaming girls!

If a guy is coming into an interaction, you should immediately introduce yourself, make him like you and then find out who he is in relation to the girls. If he is the boyfriend of the target and you want to leave the group, it's always good to ask how long they have been going out. Make them feel good before you leave. You don't ever want to be the guy that leaves just as soon as he finds out the girl isn't single.

BREAKING RAPPORT

Along with challenges (see next chapter), breaking rapport is one of the most powerful things you can do to build attraction. I include it in the optional and advanced techniques because I was able to achieve good results without them. However, when you add these to your game you'll see another dramatic improvement.

Breaking rapport is disagreeing with her on a point or expressing a contrary view. It can be very powerful. To exemplify its importance, imagine being a hot woman for a moment. You are being approached by smiling, nodding men, and feel you can't do or say anything wrong. You could say you love cats, and they will say they love cats; you can say you like torturing cats and they'll say, "Cool."

Okay, maybe that's going too far, but we all know that the natural thing to do when you're with a beautiful woman is to go into 'me too' mode, where you agree with her on everything and try to connect. The point is that you think similarities will bring you closer. This might generally be true, however, but this is what ninety-nine per cent of men do, and what you've probably realised from reading this book is that it's what ninety-nine per cent of men *don't* do that brings you success.

Imagine being that beautiful woman again. Men will agree with you on everything and think everything you do is just great. You know there are things they shouldn't like about you, but they don't express it. This means you won't fully trust them, you'll think they are only after one thing and their compliments won't be worth as much.

The answer to this is to break rapport, but you mustn't do it on big things that have an emotional connection for her. Don't call her passion for painting lame, but you can break it on casual interests like Harry Potter books, Hugh Grant films, etc. When you say that something she likes sucks, it makes it twice as powerful when you later say that you appreciate something about her.

If you say, "Oh I love Harry Potter too," "Oh yes, I love musicals," and then say, "I have a good feeling about you, we should meet again," you come off as fake. Better to say, "Harry Potter – I couldn't even get halfway through the first book," "I caught *The Lion King* but wouldn't see another musical any time soon," and then, "I love your laugh." The compliment

199

has much stronger effect, because you have shown that you only say what you mean and mean what you say.

When to break rapport

Do it after the hook point, just enough to show that she can do something wrong and lose you. The point is not to lower her self-esteem or make her feel stupid, it's just to show that you can disagree and that you have your own views and opinions. If you break rapport, the best thing to do is quickly change subject to avoid turning it into an argument.

Don't be afraid to tell the truth, it actually increases trust and connection as well as dialling up attraction. Trust and honesty are keys to gaining people's respect. This is a way to be honest without hurting people's feelings. If you notice yourself me-tooing and not getting as much attraction as you'd like after the hook point, try breaking rapport combined with genuine compliments – and also try challenges.

CHALLENGES

Challenges are ways to establish that you're the selector, the high-value one in the interaction. You choose her, not the other way around. Most guys will passively let themselves be selected, so if you can challenge her it'll be uniquely attractive. You need to have earned some value before she'll respond and try to meet your challenges. Some examples are:

• "If everyone looked the same, how would you stand out?"

- "Can you cook?"
- "Are you rich?"
- "Beauty is common, so what do you have to make me more and more attracted as I get to know you?"
- "There are three things I look for in a woman. The first is [*insert quality, e.g. confidence*], the second is [*passion*] and the third is . . . no, I'm not telling you." "Why?" "You might fake it."

The above examples communicate that you're picky and won't date just any girl – looks are not enough. This makes you more attractive because you're subconsciously telling her you're high value. This is the outer-game way to challenge a girl. The problem is that, if the thoughts in your mind are about how much you want her and how you'd do anything for her, there will be conflict between your non-verbal and verbal communication. Women are sensitive and will pick up on things subconsciously; they might not mention them or even consciously know that they have noticed, but it will affect your chances if you use this shallow means of challenging. The best way to challenge a woman is to follow the next mission:

MISSION EIGHT

Get a pen and describe your ideal woman. What character attributes would she have? Would she smoke? Does she keep fit? Can she dance? Can she sing? Is she sharp? Is she educated? Does she read poetry or *OK!* magazine? Does she like Disney films or action films? Does she like sushi? Is she well travelled? Does she watch *Sex and the City*?

If you have this in mind, when you meet a woman you won't give her as much credit for her looks, and if you can work these questions into the interaction you will flip the dynamic. She will have to start qualifying herself to you. You are positioning yourself as the selector, and seeing if she matches up to your requirements. Ninety-nine per cent of men don't do this, and you'll see how women start chasing you if you do.

Challenges with a hint of NLP

These are statements that get her to agree to your preferred behaviour. They can include subtle language and cues that link the behaviour to being with you. (You can decide what you want and make your own.) Check out the NLP section for more info on using it in a pick-up. The following are examples:

- Are you decisive? Do you know what you want when it's right in front of you? (*Point at yourself as you say this to trigger her subconscious.*) Imagine what it would be like to get it and then go for it without hesitation. Or do you let opportunities slip away? (*Lean back as you say the last part, to show her she could lose you; it subtly affects her subconscious mind.*)

- Can you be crazy and spontaneous? Do you ever do something that you know will be an amazing

202

experience that might not be logical, or somthing other people would approve of, but is what your heart is telling you to do? With me, I think those kinds of actions lead to (*point to self to indicate she should go with you*) the happiest memories and all kinds of possibilities. We have to live more in the moment, follow our feelings and enjoy things when the opportunities present themselves.

INTENSE SEXUAL ESCALATION – SENSING A WOMAN'S RESPONSIVENESS

How do you have a super-rapid sexual escalation, the kind that blows people's minds? By getting a kiss in the daytime within two minutes, or in the club after ten seconds? So how do you take a girl home after five minutes? The answer is intense sexual escalation.

Most guys go for the kiss or for sex when it's *obvious*. They wait until it's as plain as day. Let's say a girl is ready to kiss after three minutes; then I will kiss her dead on three minutes. Other guys wait six, ten, twenty minutes, or never kiss her. By pushing the boundary, you learn exactly where it is. Sometimes you'll be too early, but that's the only way to learn. All the guys that play it safe miss the point at which the switch flips in her brain. To feel it, you have to know at which point she is open to the next stage in the escalation. Otherwise it's all guesswork or waiting for something very blatant. The side benefit is that you'll even learn how to *force* the signal that she is ready, because you know what you've done in the past to trigger it. In the end, it all becomes intuitive and helps you project energy.

OBJECTION MANAGEMENT AND THE BOYFRIEND

In your mission to attract, you're going to get plenty of objections from girls. How you deal with these is very important. Many objections are just tests to see if you're enough of a man. It's more a case of presenting an attitude than learning lines. But, by looking at these examples, you can develop the right mental frame to come up with your own objection responses.

The boyfriend

HC: "I have a boyfriend."

PUA: "Cool, he can make us breakfast in bed." or

PUA: "You've a bore-friend?" or

PUA: "Good, it'll give you something to do when I'm busy." or

PUA: "Excellent, he can hang out with my girlfriend when we are together." or

PUA: "Nice. Anyway . . . [*continue seduction*]."

I should add the disclaimer here that you shouldn't mess up people's relationships lightly. You'll be treading on dangerous ground. I personally haven't messed up a good relationship, and there are no girls out there that hate me for breaking their heart. My morals mean I get laid less than I might otherwise, but I can genuinely say I love women and don't want to hurt them unnecessarily. Having said that, there are a few types of girls with boyfriends:

The first type of girl acts like she is single! You might ask if she has a boyfriend and she says yes. However, she is grinding on you, expressing interest and showing no compunction whatsoever about flirting. She is obviously not in a relationship that she cares about.

The second type still shows signs of interest but is kind of torn, and will often act nervous and unpredictable because she wants you but doesn't really want to cheat. This girl is not in an amazing relationship, but likes the guy and has morals. She can easily be persuaded by slowly building comfort and staying far away from the subject. If you take this girl, you need to consider whether you're doing the right thing because, unlike girl number one, she probably wouldn't cheat with just any guy.

The third type is the rarest of them all. It took me a few hundred approaches before I encountered this kind of girl. She has fun with you, laughs and you have a great interaction. *But* there is absolutely no sexual tension or indicators of interest. She is not looking at you in that way at all, you might as well be gay or a girl. The reason she can do this is that she is in a very solid relationship. She knows that no man can show her more in thirty minutes than her boyfriend has in the months or years that they have been together. Even if you're better looking, funnier and tick every box, she is just not thinking along those lines at all. This is a very nice girl, you want one like this for yourself when you develop a proper relationship. They are rare and you won't find many in clubs.

I have an intuition about these three types now. I can usually tell how long a girl has been in a relationship, how solid it is, and give very accurate cold reads on their relationship. I remember an approach I was making when she told me she had a boyfriend. I said, "And I have a girlfriend; she isn't here"; then I said, "Come here," and kissed her. She slapped me lightly, told me I was bad, then came and kissed me again.

Another time, I was with a girl who was showing lots of interest but seemed really nervous. It didn't make sense, and then it hit me – she had a BF, but wanted me! I gave her a great cold read: "Two-month relationship, likes him, but not that much; when she is with him she enjoys herself, but she isn't really thinking about him much now." It was spot on, and we hooked up too.

Once I was talking to a very hot girl; I ran amazing game, was getting lots of positive response, but there was no sexual element there at all. I just said, "You have a boyfriend, don't you?" and I was spot on. Students have seen me steal a girl from a date in a club as a demo, but in a situation like this I won't rock any boats unless she is my dream girl.

Rude responses

If the girl is completely rude, blanks you, or maybe her friends are very aggressive, there are only two ways to deal with the situation. You can defuse it with a comment like, "Wow, you're so cute when you're mad," or "Whoa, is she your bodyguard? You should take her to one of these places with all big rugby guys and get her to harshly reject all of them," or "Wow, that was so cool, the way you blew me out. Do it again. Look, I'm gonna do my best chat-up line this time. I wasn't bringing my A-game before!" Or you can just be silent and leave.

I would never advocate being rude or insulting a girl, whatever she does. A girl has a right not to want to speak to you. She even has a right to be in a bad mood sometimes, or to hate men. It's better to give her this right than to hate her for it. Love women, enjoy the good interactions, and don't let the bad ones bother you.

SEXUAL SPIKES

Often, you can just physically escalate the kino to get her primed for the kiss close. But you can also use verbal escalation to get her in the mood and bring in some sexual tension. Most guys won't do it, or at least won't do it smoothly. Here are some routines and lines that can be used:

- "Cool, you're my new girlfriend."
- "You look like you're imagining kissing me." This is a

good one, because it isn't asking if she wants to kiss you, but if she responds positively the kiss is on. If she wasn't imagining kissing you already, she will after this. Watch her look at your lips! Then you could say, "Okay, now you are."

- "[*take pulse*] I knew it, you are attracted to me."
- When you're having a conversation, stop, look at her boobs. Check them out blatantly. When she asks, "What are you doing?" or calls you on it, put a finger up to signal 'wait', then look up and say, "Okay, carry on." It's very funny.
- "What is your favourite fruit? Wow, I have never eaten [*strawberries*] off a naked woman before!"
- "The other day, I heard the craziest chat-up line, a guy said, 'Imagine me going down on you all night,' now I don't know about you, but . . ."
- "How much would you like to kiss me?"
- "On a scale of one to ten, how dirty is your mind?"
- "If you were in kissing school, what grade would you get? Let's find out!"

NLP FOR SEDUCTION

Using NLP in the seduction involves using language in particular ways to generate attraction, create a connection, evoke feelings in the girl and attach them to you.

Eliciting emotions

The key to using speed seduction effectively is eliciting emotions from the girl. A girl who doesn't feel anything when she is with you will not easily be won over. The quickest way to make her feel something is to bring out past memories that have strong emotions connected to them. Doing this is simpler than creating them from scratch. So what might you do? Ask questions like:

- Do you remember the last time you were in love?
- Have you ever felt completely comfortable with a man who you trust?
- Could you imagine what it would be like to have someone love you completely and totally?
- When was the last time you had really amazing sex?
- When was the last time you felt amazingly aroused?

Anchoring

Anchoring is the act of linking something, usually a touch, to a particular feeling in the girl. The theory is that you can trigger the anchored feeling at a future time by re-firing the anchor. When the girl is feeling the peak of that particular emotion, touch her in a certain place, for example her elbow, and remember that when you re-fire it you'll need to touch the same place with the same pressure.

Matching and mirroring

When you're with your close friends, you'll do things like use the same buzzwords, make the same gestures and speak at a similar pace. By spending time with these people you have become in sync with them. Maybe you were drawn to them in the first place because of their similarity to you. You can create this artificially with a stranger, making them feel closer to you and more comfortable with you. To achieve this, match/mirror:

- Voice speed – speak at the same speed as them.
- Voice tone – match voice tone.
- Posture – match the way they sit or stand.
- Gestures – emulate gestures
- Common words – if they say 'fantastic' a lot, make it part of your vocabulary.
- Match their rate of breathing.

Pacing and leading

This is the art of matching a mood or state, and then leading into another one. If someone is tired and you approach with guns blazing, they'll be resistant. It's better to match their low-energy mood for a while, then slowly and smoothly lift your own state and they will follow. Besides low-energy people, pacing and leading can be used to subtly take a hyper girl down a few notches, or relax someone who is stressed.

Embedded commands

Embedded commands involve the use of sentences within sentences that act on the subconscious mind and direct the girl towards a particular goal. The words are emphasised with a subtle change in tonality, and an example would be, "Do you ever *feel completely relaxed, now* and then I find that . . ." This sentence will command the girl to "feel completely relaxed" and will not be rejected because it is hidden within a longer sentence.

Patterns

Seduction patterns are scripted pieces of speech which are designed to lead a girl in a particular direction, and usually combine all of the above elements to produce a powerful effect. An example of a pattern would be:

"Have you ever just met someone and almost immediately you *start to feel incredibly comfortable*, like you've known this person forever and then, as you *just let the barriers drop* and you let them more inside, you start to naturally feel a sense of rightness, like this is meant to be?"

NLP patterns can be used effectively in almost any interaction, but are best suited for a quiet environment with few distractions, or when you're already in a comfortable one-on-one situation with a girl.

COLD READING

This is a powerful technique. Everyone loves being told about themselves. Women are especially susceptible, and palm readers will tell you that a huge percentage of their customers are female. Cold reading can be learned in five minutes, and women will go mad for it. It also builds good rapport, because you're showing understanding. A woman who thinks she has found someone who finally understands her will be very happy!

There are two methods I use to cold read. You can either buy a bunch of books on the subject or just read this, practise and then be better than most professional 'psychics'.

Agreeable statements

The first thing I do is use statements that pretty much anyone will agree with. Here are some examples:

- "You're generally liked by others and enjoy being around people you like. But, at times, you feel the need to be alone with your thoughts and have time to yourself with no interruptions."

- "You can generally be trusted, and I'd say that perhaps you're a little more honest than most people."

- "You're generally content with the way things have worked out for you, but sometimes you wonder if you should take a chance and try something completely different, the kind of thing that would surprise people that have known you a long time."

- "You might feel you have a lot of unused capacity. That people don't always give you full credit for your abilities. Some of your hopes and goals tend to be far off or unrealistic. You're independent and original. You don't just accept what people tell you to believe. You like to find your own reasons to support an action."

212

As you can see, these are things you can just trot out and most people will nod along to. Tailor them to your own method of speaking and vocabulary. You are supposed to be openly communicating, so don't make it sound rehearsed. Women are much more susceptible than men to this stuff, so even if you think it wouldn't work on you it'll probably work on a girl.

The power of 'but' and 'and'

The second method of cold reading is one that I prefer. It's using subjects that split people fifty-fifty to tell someone about themselves. You start with viewpoint A and, if it looks like you're wrong, you save it before they really notice and then tell them how much they are like B, and you expand on B so much that they forget you ever mentioned A. Let me give an example I used on a girl:

"I think you might be quite outgoing and like to meet new people [*shows disapproval*], but on the other hand you don't find this kind of thing easy. You prefer one-on-one interactions with close friends rather than a big group. You enjoy really getting to know someone and having deep conversations, rather than the kind of casual stuff that happens when you put a big group together. I think you also enjoy time by yourself and like to be alone with your thoughts. You then come back refreshed, with a clear sense of what you're doing."

Okay, so in the above I start off with a fifty-fifty chance of success. In practice, other clues she gives you will greatly increase that. But, assuming a fifty-fifty chance, you either get it right from the get-go or you make an initial mistake. If you make a mistake, you use the word 'but' or something similar and go the opposite way. It works well, because you then use 'and' to add more and more detail to that picture and then it seems like you're getting ninety-five per cent right, but in fact each additional point is one that naturally follows from acceptance of the first.

Subjects for cold reading

You can split people down the middle on subjects like these:

- Introvert/extrovert.
- Politics – left/right.
- Likes exercising/doesn't.
- Creative/logical.
- Emotional/logical.
- Trusting/untrusting.
- Belief in paranormal, etc.,/scientific.

There are hundreds of others. Using the above and practising it is the best way to learn. On a boot-camp, we can normally teach good cold-reading skills in just twenty minutes.

PUSH PULL

Push pull is great because it accomplishes a couple of things:
- It establishes you as high value – other guys wouldn't dare do this!
- It gives her an emotional rollercoaster ride, a necessary ingredient for a great pick-up.

Here are some examples of lines you can use for this effect:
- "You're like my bratty little sister."
- "Do you have hot friends?"
- "Would you like me to buy you a drink?"
- "You're too young/old for me."
- "Wow, you ask loads of questions, do you want my resume?"
- "You're a nice girl with bad-girl mannerisms."
- "You're a bad girl with nice-girl mannerisms."
- "Normally I'd be really attracted to you, but I think you're just acting cool so I'll buy you a drink."
- "Your first impression kind of sucked, but actually . . ."
- "You're the coolest girl I've talked to . . . in the last fifteen minutes!"
- "You're cool . . . you can help me pick up chicks."

DANCE-FLOOR GAME

Can you pick up girls on the dance-floor? If you don't, you're limiting yourself. There are a whole load of girls who love dancing that you won't be able to approach. My philosophy was that I wanted to be able to pick up a girl I was attracted to at any time, in any place and any situation. As someone with two left feet, I felt uncomfortable in clubs and was very self-conscious; dance-floor game didn't come easy. Now I can dance a little bit – at least I'm on beat – but the main thing is that I am not self-conscious and I have fun dancing. I actually enjoy it!

There are a few ways to pick up a girl on the dance-floor. It will always be more of a numbers game because it's non-verbally direct. First you need to differentiate yourself from the other guys on the dance-floor. They are doing a couple of things that you should not do. They are either:

- Standing around the girls, checking them out while not dancing.
- Making a sad attempt to dance whilst not being into the music, just trying to get near the girls.
- Grinding on a girl's ass.

Here are some things you can do to pick up on the dance-floor:

- Have fun dancing around; don't try to get near the woman. Enjoy yourself, enjoy the music. When you're a man having fun on the dance-floor, you'll immediately stand out from all the other men. The women will move away from all the other guys and gather around you.
- You can then mirror the girls dancing in an exaggeratedly funny way, get eye contact and force

interest, have a 'dance-off' with the girl where you gesture to her to watch your moves, bust a silly little move and then point at her expectantly.

- On the edge of the dance-floor with girls that are not quite dancing, you can say, "Do you like dancing?" If they say yes, say, "Do you salsa?" and, as you say it, take them and start salsaing. You need about four salsa lessons to be able to do the basic steps, which are all you need. You can quickly kino-escalate from the salsa opener.

The goal on the dance-floor is to dance with them, escalate kino a little and then extract to a quieter location where you can talk.

Inner Game

FEELING GOOD ABOUT YOURSELF, STAYING MOTIVATED AND FOCUSED: TOOLS OF THE TRADE

THE FIRST THING ANYONE WHO WANTS TO SUCCEED IN THIS AREA SHOULD DO IS USE A NOTEBOOK. The notebook should contain various things and, if used properly, will allow you to feel good about yourself, have a clear understanding of what you're doing and keep you motivated and positive. It should also contain the following sections:

1. Affirmations (see next subsection).
2. Concise notes on everything you learn about attraction — whether from self-improvement books, other people or your own observations. Keep these concise. If you can't summarise the average self-help book in six lines, then you need to work on this.

3. A list of things you want to try out in the field – openers, routines, whatever.

4. A breakdown of your interactions; what went well, what went badly and what you should do next time to make it better. Even if you close, you could have probably closed earlier. It's possible to close while only doing it thirty per cent right. Analysing your interactions will be a great way to improve quickly.

5. A month-by-month summary of your progress. Example: "July: Read *The Natural Art of Seduction*. Number closed HC Spanish, HC Swedish, first k-close using game, 20 approaches every Friday. August: k-closed HC French, HC Anna, HC Emily, first day-game number close . . ."

This summary should be short; it's not like a diary, it's just a quick record of the interactions. What it does is allow you to look back and feel good about the progress you're making. As with anything, you'll have setbacks on a day-to-day basis, but you'll be able to recover from them if you can see a pattern of progress. It also forces you to judge your own progress instead of other people's. You can always find someone with more women, more money, more material possessions, but, as long as you judge only yourself and your own progress, you'll be satisfied. Keeping a record of it means you won't forget where you came from, and you can be proud of yourself every time you look back.

Crib sheet

In the early days, it helps to carry around something with summaries of everything you know. You can even refer to it when you get stuck, by going to the bathroom and then coming back with an idea of what you need to do. Mine contained:

1. My affirmations (for mental state).
2. A list of openers.
3. Demonstrations of higher value.
4. Cocky or funny lines.
5. Seduction routines.

AFFIRMATIONS

This is what I recommend people use for both state control and long-term change. Affirmations are positive statements made about yourself that act on your subconscious mind. Over time they affect your self-image, confidence and beliefs. You can test the effectiveness of affirmations by writing a list of all the things you like about yourself on one side of a piece of paper and all the things you don't like about yourself on the other side. Notice how your mood is affected differently when you read each side. By writing and using positive affirmations, you're counteracting the generally negative influences that other people, the media and society in general have on your self-esteem.

Some books suggest you read affirmations out loud in

front of a mirror twice a day. I don't think you need to go that far; you can keep them in your notebook and read them before you go on a date, or any other time it suits you to be in a positive state. You can also record your affirmations on to an MP3 and play them on a loop for hours. That would be a sure-fire way to get them deep into your subconscious. It's important to follow these rules when writing your affirmations. Otherwise, they just won't be as effective:

1. A positive statement written in the present tense: "I am friendly." *Not* "I will be friendly."

2. No use of negative words: "I'm not an idiot," should be, "I'm clever." "I don't get rejected," should be, "All women love me." The subconscious doesn't understand negatives; that's why, if you generally use phrases such as "not too good" instead of "bad", you'll be healthier in your outlook. The classic NLP example is to tell you to think of anything except a pink elephant. You have just thought of a pink elephant, so saying, "I'm not a loser who gets rejected and everyone hates," is just as bad as saying, "I *am* a loser who gets rejected and everyone hates."

3. The affirmations should be based on how you picture your ideal self. The person you'd like to be. You at your best.

4. They should make you feel something when you say them. If they don't, change the language around or scrap it.

You can write affirmations as statements and in a paragraph form. Below are some sample examples. However, please be sure to make yours meaningful to yourself. I wrote my first affirmations in mid-2003 – they all came true within a couple of years! At the time they were outside the realm of possibility, but I believe my subconscious helped me make them a reality. Now I've written some next-level affirmations and I hope they come true, too.

Examples:

- I am friendly.
- I am fun-loving.
- I am approachable.
- I am interesting.
- I am clever.
- I am a leader.
- I am challenging.
- I am a success in all that I do.
- I can attract any woman I want.
- I know my purpose.
- I am confident about who I am.
- I am an attractive man.
- I have a powerful reality.
- I am cool, calm, collected.
- My world and my life are attractive and interesting.
- People like me, they want to meet me.
- I am very interested in other people.
- I want to meet fun, positive and interesting people.

UNIVERSAL FRAME

I am high status

Status is something that's often talked about in the pick-up community, but is rarely well defined or presented in a practical manner. Yet it's very important. Whether it's with friends, at work or with a girl, one person is of higher status than the rest. This person is the decision maker, the one who is deferred to by the group. Are you the one who asks, "Think we should go to X place?" If so, you're low status. You're handing over the decision-making power to someone else. If you say, "Let's go to X place," and everyone follows, you're the group's high-status person. If your friend always ends phone conversations first, he is of higher status than you. Examples of high status are all around us, and visible in the media. A high-status person never gives away power to someone else. He never defers. He doesn't seek approval. He doesn't ask for permission.

The more beautiful the woman, the more she's used to being given all the status. A man will ask her to make decisions on everything, from whether it's okay to take her number and when she's available to meet, to where she would like to go, whether his clothes are okay and if the food is good. This is actually very unattractive. It's so common for men to give away all their power like this that the rare man who doesn't is prized.

Though I gave the example of status with your friends and work colleagues, there is no point in attempting to change the dynamic with these people. It might jeopardise these relationships. I am happy to play beta and low status with good friends. But, with women, it's simply unattractive.

Status is mainly communicated through the choice of words. Use this combination with women: let your words be borderline rude while lovingly looking at her and touching her. This mix will allow you to avoid her thinking you're too cocky and will be very attractive. The rules for maintaining status when dealing with women are:

1. Don't ask lots of questions.
2. Don't give her the decision-making power. Only give her the option to accept your choices: "Where would you like to eat?" gives her the decision-making power, but, "Let's go to the Italian, yeah?" just gives her the chance to go along with your decision.
3. Don't seek approval: "Is this okay?" "Is that all right with you?" "How's my jacket look?"
4. Lead: "I'm hungry, let's go eat." "I'm thirsty, let's go get a drink."

FRAME OF MIND DURING AN INTERACTION

Here is an attractive mindset for interaction with women:

- I am the most important person in this relationship.
- What she says doesn't matter.
- Don't do anything that would make her think, "What a wuss!"
- All women want me.

- She is hitting on me.
- Everything she does is cute: "Wow, look at her face when she's mad, so cute!"
- I'm super hot and all women want me.
- She is hot. Okay, but what else does she have going for her?
- I'm a super-cool guy; can she see that or is she a dunce?
- Assume the close.
- Everything she does is a sign of interest.

FRAME OF MIND IN A RELATIONSHIP

How does an attractive man act once he is dating a girl or in a relationship? The following are some principles of attractive male behaviour:

1. **Don't ask too many questions.** An unattractive man is always wondering if things are okay and if the girl is happy; it conveys approval-seeking, weakness, neediness, all the bad stuff. An attractive man can still look for signs from the girl and adjust his behaviour accordingly; he's not rude, but he assumes things are fine and is generally comfortable.

2. **Lead, make decisions and surprise her.** This is very important. The man needs to be leading. Questions like this should be avoided: "Where would you like to go tonight?" "What would you like to do today?" "What film shall we watch?" "What do you want to do for your birthday?" Putting the decision-making

power on the woman gives her higher status and takes away yours. It is not being nice, or polite, or equal; it is being boring and unattractive. Women love to be led around and to be surprised, so do it! Examples: "I'm hungry, let's go eat." "Let's go and watch a film." "Wear casual clothes, we are doing something active!"

3. **Send mixed messages and make her work.** This is about being less attainable and remaining a challenge. Don't have lots of long phone conversations, call every day, text her all day long, send loads of emails or try to see her every day. When you are with her, give her your all. When you are apart, get on with your life. The attraction builds when you have stuff to do and she has to work for you. Again, it's not being rude, it's being a man. Don't chase her, and the frame of the relationship will change. As long as she has to work for you, she'll always be interested.

4. **Don't change yourself for her.** There are going to be things about you she doesn't like. Some she will have a good reason for. If she does, and you agree, change them. If she doesn't like your clothes, music, hobbies, friends, but you do, *do not* change for her. When a woman has changed a man into her ideal, she becomes bored and will look for the next project! It's part of why she wants the bad boy; she wonders if she could be the one who tames him.

INNER GAME LAWS

1. Make your frame of reference internal

A major source of unhappiness in most people's lives is discontentment caused by comparing ourselves with others. We see the man with a Ferrari, beautiful girlfriend or great lifestyle and we feel envious. The fact is, if you compare yourself with other people, you'll *always* be unhappy. There is always someone with more money, more women, better looks, whatever. I used to judge myself by other people, trying to beat them, and was never content. Now I can say that my frame of reference is pretty much internal and I am much happier for it. What this means is that you judge yourself by yourself only. Let's say you used to have no women at all, and now you can get numbers and dates. That's something to be proud of and happy about. Judged by yourself, you've made good progress. If you want to feel bad, you can look at the guy who sleeps with five women a week and still isn't happy.

In pick-up terms, the best way to make your frame of reference internal is to:

- Keep track of your progress – have a written record of where you're at each month so you can chart the progress. I do this, and any time I have a setback or want to judge myself by someone else, I can look at this. I'll see the great progress I've made and I'll be happy.

- Make plans for the future. Record your goals and each step necessary to get there. Make it happen. If you're uncertain and don't have direction, this allows you to focus on other people.

- Cut down on watching TV and unhealthy social influences. If you watch MTV all day, it's selling a life that's not real and that 99.99 per cent of people can't have. You want to live like Hugh Hefner? That will make you unsatisfied even if you have a beautiful girl – *if* you let it!

- Remember that everyone has strengths and weaknesses. Just because someone is richer doesn't mean they are happier; in fact, they probably are not. The guy with the Ferrari probably works twelve hours a day, or was born rich so he doesn't get satisfaction from having earned it. Most people will have something you *could* be envious of. But remember, if your goal is to be a well-rounded, contented human being, this shouldn't bother you.

2. Eliminate the concept of failure

When you go out and start approaching women, you'll make mistakes. There is no way to fully prepare for every eventuality before you go out. Expect to make mistakes. What is important is how you deal with them. When you make a mistake, learn from it and know what you should do in the future. What you can say is: "I'm glad I made that mistake. Now that I've learned from it, I'll never mess up in that situation again." Most of the pain of failure is caused by the belief that you can fail like that again. If you write down what happened, what you should have done and how you'll avoid it happening again, then you'll immediately feel better. Remember that the average millionaire entrepreneur has a string of failed businesses behind him. The average PUA has hundreds of blow-outs and rejections behind him. The guy that goes out and does a hundred approaches that day and gets blown out eighty times is still better than the guy who only does two but picks his shots. He will learn much more, losing his inhibitions and fear in the process. Plus he'll gain way more numbers, dates, kisses, sex, girlfriends, and whatever else he wants.

3. Surround yourself with success models

It's useful to be influenced by people that have qualities you would like for yourself. For me, I needed to learn how to be a sociable extrovert. All my old friends are like me, so hanging out with them only reinforced my old habits. If you want to change, you need to hang around with people who have qualities that you lack. After I hung around extroverts for a while, I became more outgoing and gained the skills that made them good socially. Now, if I lack a quality, I know that the best way to get it is to find someone with it and learn from them. If you have trouble finding people that you admire, read books, watch videos and listen to audio by or about people like David Deangelo (dating advice) and Tony Robbins (self-help), who are great motivational figures.

There are many examples of people who led amazing lives that can inspire you. You can read about them and it will motivate you to become the best that you can. My favourites:

- Nikola Tesla, the genius inventor who was decades ahead of his time.
- Thomas Edison, who was told by a discouraged assistant, after having performed some 50,000 tests without success, "You must be pretty downhearted with the lack of progress." Edison replied, "Downhearted? We've made a lot of progress. At least we know 50,000 things that won't work!" In the end he developed a nickel–iron alkaline battery that became an industry standard, and is still used today – more than ninety years later!
- Sportspeople like Lance Armstrong, the cyclist who overcame cancer and won the Tour De France seven years in a row.

4. Surround yourself with positive people

When we are embarking on a period of change in our life, we will be moving away from our social circle and will begin acting differently and changing before our friends' eyes. This can cause a lot of problems. Most people stay the same and don't improve. These people will reinforce your bad habits and bad behaviour. It's like being a drug addict and being around other drug addicts. They reinforce your bad behaviour and will not encourage you to change. When you start to become good with women, your friends can hold you back. A big percentage of people are negative and will find problems with all your new ideas. Even if someone is a good friend, you need to be careful about the effect they have on your mental state. The way to judge is this: if you spend an hour with this person, do you feel better or worse about things? If you feel worse, cut down the time spent. Similarly to the above, if you lack positive people you can bring them into your life by studying great role models throughout history.

5. Use the time when you're not picking up – awareness and ideas

An important PUA skill is the ability to be aware. What is a sign of interest and what isn't? Who is a couple? Who is out looking for a man? When you're in a social situation, look around, make your best guess and then try to verify it. Over time, awareness of social situations allows you to know exactly where you stand in an interaction.

The second thing you can do is to be anywhere – supermarket, bookshop, train station – and imagine what you would use to open a transition. Don't wait until you see a beautiful woman to start thinking of things that you could say. Walk around and think of situational openers to exercise your mental muscles, even use them on women you don't find attractive to practise being a spontaneous, sociable guy.

6. Balance learning, practising and refining

Some people spend twelve months going through the theory. There are enough ebooks, videos and audio products for you to stay in your house forever and still think you're doing something useful. I actually made this mistake for a few months, I went through thousands of hours of study before I really tried anything in the field. Practising is the hardest part, that's why it's the most important thing to do *now*. I learned more from two weeks of going out than I did with my months of theory.

Some people *just* go out. They don't refine their approach and don't learn any new techniques. These people usually don't improve very rapidly. The best approach is to learn some theory (as you now have!) and go out and practise (like tonight!). Then come back, look at what you did and refine it. Rinse, repeat. Now you have the best and most efficient method to improve quickly.

7. Stop idealising women and relationships

Most men put women on a pedestal, they give them a lot of credit for their looks and would commit to a date, a relationship, or maybe even more, purely based on this. Most women are not right for you! Likewise, most relationships don't work! Adopting these as new beliefs will enable you to approach more confidently and be more circumspect.

8. Eliminate all nervous tics and unattractive mannerisms
It is important to be aware of how you look at all times.

Ask your friends to tell you about the things you do that are unattractive or stupid. I used to have a nervous laugh, bite my lip, touch my face and fidget, amongst other things.

9. Learn how to make a conversation interesting for a woman

VISUALISATION TECHNIQUES

These are something that can be used very effectively to improve your pick-up skills. They allow you to field test openers and routines in a controlled environment. You need to be in a very relaxed state, because a fully conscious and aware state has too many distractions. Likewise, field-testing openers in a live situation is very good, but there are lots of things trying to grab your attention. Visualisation will allow you to come up with new material, to see what will or won't work, and practise your delivery. The process is as follows:

Get into a very relaxed state using self-hypnosis. If you've never tried self-hypnosis, what you need to do is to breathe deeply, take your focus of attention into your body and notice the sensations throughout. Close your eyes. A good time to do this is just before you sleep.

Think of an opener and transition that you would like to field-test. Imagine an approach, and watch yourself deliver your opener. See their response. Watch how you'll respond to their response, and let the interaction flow.

233

OVERCOMING TRANSITION AND APPROACH ANXIETY

Transition anxiety

When doing something outside your comfort zone, you'll naturally find it scary. Transition anxiety is best described as the feeling you get in your stomach at any time like this. Whether it's the thought of riding a scary rollercoaster, jumping out of a plane, signing up for a course, meeting new people at a party, taking a test, public speaking or approaching a woman: what all these things share in common is that they may give us butterflies in our stomach, to varying degrees.

This feeling is holding us back; it doesn't serve us well. Anything that's outside of our comfort zone, that we haven't done before or that puts us in an uncertain situation that we don't feel equipped for will cause some transition anxiety. That would be fine if the feeling was saving us from getting eaten by a lion or doing something hazardous, *but* it's actually only stopping us from improving, learning and changing.

We have a comfort zone within which we can safely stay inside – a daily routine, people we know. However, remaining in this comfort zone makes it hard to make big changes or improvements to your life. If you look back and remember all the times you've felt transition anxiety and taken action anyway, you'll see that each time it has impacted your life in a positive way. Whether it was moving to a new area, changing job, taking a class, signing up for a course, they will likely be things that have benefited you greatly. A man who decides to get a handle on this area of his life will feel transition anxiety before he clicks the sign-up button on the website. Lots of others will feel it and never click the button. It's a fact!

So what about those crazy people who always try new things and never feel uncomfortable? If anything, they welcome uncertain new situations. They have changed that feeling in their stomach from something that holds them back to something that kicks them into action. This is what I have done. I used to be a complete scaredy cat when it came to almost anything that involved leaving my house! Now, any time I get that feeling, I know that I should take action and that, by the end of it, I'll be a better person. As a result, fewer and fewer things intimidate me and I feel like I can handle almost anything. Embrace transition anxiety and you'll be thanking me later. It will affect every area of your life and will make you a better person.

Approach anxiety

Approaching a woman you're attracted to is one of the scariest things a guy can do. You know it doesn't make sense that you're as afraid to do this as you would be to fight someone who's trying to rob you. But, in one situation, the worst that can happen is that she says 'no'; in the second, the worst that can happen is serious physical injury. Over ninety-five per cent of the people I work with have some degree of approach anxiety. Conquering it is not something that NLP or affirmations can provide a quick fix for. There is no easy way to get over it. However, I can tell you the most painless way possible. In my experience, thirty approaches will be enough to free you of crippling approach anxiety. You might still have some, but you'll be opening enough groups to get along.

First, let's take away some of the fear (or 'outcome dependency'). As long as you have a lot of approach anxiety, work on that first. In your first approaches, you're not 'opening to close', you're just opening and ejecting, practising opening. Just going up, asking, "What's the time?", thanking her and leaving is a lot easier than approaching with the intention of getting her back to your place.

The next thing you can do is use indirect openers. These minimise the chance of rejection and allow you to practise opening without caring whether she's attracted or has a boyfriend. Finally, it helps not to be too fussy. Practise opening and extending the interaction, but do it with any group. Don't try to conquer your fear or practise pick-up skills only with women you find super-hot. It will take too long. You need to be out there practising, opening twenty groups a day. You have to be focused on practising, not on closing. When I began, I opened twenty a night. Now I'm fussy, and only approach particular girls who meet my standards. But that's because my skills don't need much polishing or refinement. If I had tried to improve by

236

opening only one or two a night, it would have taken ten times longer!

'Missions' can also get you over approach anxiety. Give yourself missions each time you go out. Test openers, or see how many groups you can engage. Go out with a friend and push each other into action. Find out what your motivation is and when you perform well. I perform well under pressure, so it's good to tell the guys I'll open any group they want me to. Other people might want to dare or bet each other. Find out what will make your approach happen. Some guys do better with a wing, so experiment.

FRAMING AN UNCOMFORTABLE SITUATION

Some situations just feel uncomfortable. Approaching a girl you really fancy, and knowing you'll be crushed if she rejects you because you haven't had sex in six months, is going to be uncomfortable. Going to a club on your own probably will be too. However, most of the discomfort from these situations has to do with your mental frame. By framing a situation differently, you can actually be at ease. I have done this for self-conscious people on my one-on-one trainings. I get them to stand for one minute in a very busy street and look straight ahead, no fidgeting, no shifting around, no looking down. They inevitably feel uncomfortable, like everyone is looking at them. I then tell them to repeat the exercise, imagining that a friend of theirs is going to appear in the distance around the corner and that they're waiting to go have coffee with him. They do it again and it's usually completely comfortable for them.

Similarly, being alone in a club can be framed so that you're completely comfortable – you're waiting for a friend. You were meant to meet at the entrance, he texted to say he is running late and will be there in an hour. Now you can be more comfortable in the club on your own, though nothing has really changed. It's like method acting.

You can also apply this to approaching women. Instead of having a pick-up frame in your head, you should have, "I'm a fun, sociable guy, I'm going to talk to lots of people, and, if I happen to have a good interaction with a girl who I find attractive, closing will be natural." This is a much healthier frame and also removes a lot of the approach anxiety, outcome dependency and neediness. You should try to reframe any situation in which you feel uncomfortable.

Closing Thoughts

M Y JOURNEY OVER THE PAST SIX YEARS HAS BEEN INTERESTING, CHALLENGING AND FUN. I'VE FELT ALMOST AS GOOD ON THE WAY HERE AS I DO NOW, WHEN I HAVE ACHIEVED MOST OF MY GOALS. When you plan to do something, see the ultimate goal as within reach and, when you look back at your progress, it will make you happier immediately.

Being fantastic with women is not a good ultimate goal, just like having X amount of money isn't a healthy goal. Being good with women will enable you to have choice for the rest of your life. Your ultimate goal in terms of relationships will be in there somewhere. Money allows you to do things that can enrich your life – they are the ultimate goal, not the money. It's best to take a holistic approach to both.

Keep balance in your life. Enjoy the present as much as

you can, but strive for more. When you start attaining some success, it's fine to be content and enjoy yourself. You only need that initial pain and discomfort to force you to take action.

The key to happiness throughout any long journey of self-improvement is keeping balance. At one time or another, one area of your life is going to be bad. You'll have setbacks. If you're *too* focused on PU, money, your job, your girlfriend, your studies, then they will have too much control over your mood. Bring balance to your life by working on different areas at once. When one isn't going so well, you've others to compensate.

There is no way to become great with women without suffering all kinds of pain on the way there. Dealing with this in the right way, learning from it and not letting it affect you too much, is what will make the difference. After a certain amount of discomfort, you'll come through the other side.

Use my inner-game techniques and you'll save yourself a lot of this pain. Get out there and apply the techniques in this book and you'll handle this area of your life. It really is in your hands now.

This book contains almost everything I know. I say *almost* because there are lots of other tiny titbits that wouldn't fit in. What I can tell you is that this book will give you the potential to be better with women than I am. I don't apply *all* the techniques in this book. If you do, and you have your own qualities as well, there's no telling how good you can be.

Thanks for reading. I'd welcome your thoughts/
feed-back/complaints!
Gambler@puatraining.com

CREDIT TO

David Deangelo, Tyler D, Lance Mason, Wes H,
Neil Strauss, Badboy, Hemal R, Wayne Elise, Dave Z,
Anthony P, Andi B, Steve Jabba, Cardenas, Will/Daddy,
Craig, David X, Mystery, Megadirt, Ross Jeffries

USEFUL LINKS

WWW.PUATRAINING.COM
Blog: www.puatraining.com/puablog